How Can I Forgive My Cheating Partner?

How Can I Forgive My Cheating Partner?

Annie Lane

Creators Publishing
Hermosa Beach, CA

How Can I Forgive My Cheating Partner?
Copyright © 2021 CREATORS PUBLISHING
All rights reserved. No part of this book may be reproduced or transmitted in any form or by any means, electronic or mechanical, including photocopying, recording or by any information storage and retrieval system, without permission in writing from the author.

Cover art by Alessandra Caruso

CREATORS PUBLISHING
737 3rd St
Hermosa Beach, CA 90254
310-337-7003

This book is not intended as a substitute for the medical advice of physicians or psychiatrists. The reader should consult a physician in matters relating to his or her health, particularly with respect to any symptoms that may require diagnosis or medical attention. The author and publisher do not assume and hereby disclaim any liability to any party for any loss, damage or disruption caused by errors or omissions, whether such errors or omissions result from negligence, accident or any other cause.

ISBN (print): 978-1-949673-68-5
ISBN (ebook): 978-1-949673-69-2

First Edition
Printed in the United States of America
1 3 5 7 9 10 8 6 4 2

*To everyone who has written to me.
You make this column possible.*

Contents

Old Flame Brings Problems	1
Long-Distance Distrust	2
Cold Shoulder After Divorce	3
All Not in the Family	4
Hidden Conversation	6
Writing Down What's Hard to Say Aloud	7
Shark on the Hunt	8
Gossip Leads to Nothing Good	10
Keep the Fun of Fantasy Alive	11
Wrecking a Home and a Career Opportunity	12
Moving Out and Moving On	13
Half-Truths Cause Heartbreak	14
Brother Is a Doormat	15
Cheating Pig	16
Picture Causing Worry	18
DNA Results Bombshell	19
Not-So-Sunny Marriage	20
Still Hurting After Divorce	22
35-Year-Old Surprise	23
Unforgiven Infidelity	25
Free from Expectations	27
Rebuilding After Betrayal	27
Breaking the Cycle of Guilt and Pain	29
Don't Mess with Married Men	31
Struggling to Trust Again	31
Confused Over Two-Timer	32
Infidelity in the Inbox	33
Sex Addiction Secret	35
Back-to-Back Betrayal	36
Past Stuck in Future	37
Porn Causing Divide in Marriage	38
Best to Leave It Alone	39

Be Safe; Get Tested	41
Dousing Old Flames	41
Speak Up For Sexual Health's Sake	43
Happiness Takes Work, Not Quick Fixes	44
Unwilling to Change His Cheating Ways	45
Countless Texts to Other Women	47
Looking to Demolish this Relationship	47
A Yo-Yo Relationship	48
My Husband the Creep	50
Cut the Cord	51
Working Through Emotional Affair	53
Disapproving of Affair	54
Breaking the DNA Test News	54
Your Marriage Matters Most	56
Icky Behavior	57
Time to Fully Commit or Quit	58
Don't Quit Yet	59
Hard Truths on the Hard Drive	60
Ditch the Two-Timer	61
The Only Way Back from Cheating Is Through Truth	62
Cut the Toxicity Out of Your Life	63
Wanting to Leave After So Many Lies	64
Rocky Seas Lead to Drifting Ships	65
Hidden Grief	66
Wanting to Be Happy	67
Affairs of the Heart	69
Broken After Baby	70
Suffering in Silence	71
Marriage Is More Than Being There	72
Fidelity to Facebook Over Matrimony	73
13 Years of Bad Luck	75
Fiancee's Fishy Friendship	76
Honesty Needed in a Healthy Marriage	77
You Can, and Should, Escape	78
Not Worth the Trouble	79

Couple Is Worlds Apart Before Tying the Knot	80
Lack of Faith in Long-Distance Relationship	81
The Other Women	82
Eroded Trust	84
Seeing a Married Man	85
Slept with Wife's Nieces	86
A New Beginning Up North	87
Husband Wants to Reconcile After Affair	89
Husband Talking to My Best Friend	90
Reeling from Wife's Affairs	91
Ditching the Cheating Boyfriend	93
Abuse and Another Man	94
Finding Love in All the Wrong Places	96
He's a Toad	98
Husband's Hidden Life	99
Choose and Commit	100
Boyfriend Sexting Other Women	101
Stop Playing Games	103
Ex Angry I'm Dating	104
Unfriended by my Husband	105
Stop Putting Up with a Cheater	106
Let Her Go	107
To Tell or Not	108
Endless Chain of Cheating	109
When to Move in Together	110
Don't Go Crawling Back	111
Best Friend Turned Cheating Boyfriend	112
Delusions of Infidelity	113
Gaining Pleasure Elsewhere	114
Marriage Takes Two	115
Dating My Ex-Husband	116
Gone Goodbye	117
Giving Up on Dating	119
Cheating in the Chatroom	120
Love Versus Lust	121
Regaining Trust Takes Time	122

Husband Has a Wandering Eye	123
How Do I Make It Right After Cheating on my Boyfriend?	124
A Promiscuous Former Life	125
Hung Up Over a Stupid Comment	126
Solve Your Own Relationship Issues	127
Is My Relationship Doomed?	128
Jealousy Isn't Healthy	129
Boyfriend Is Hiding Things	130
Sudden Change in Tone	131
Husband's Eyes Are Always on the Move	132
Fifty Years Unforgiven	133
Knowledge Is Power	134
Gawking Husband Is Taught a Lesson	136
Age Gap Is Inappropriate	136
Friends Need to Speak Up About Infidelity	137
Misplaced Blame For Affair	138

Author's Note

No matter how convinced you are that a letter
is about your family, any similarity to any person or
situation is purely coincidental. Names, jobs, genders, ages and
other identifying details have all been changed.
These are opinions, and they're meant
for entertainment purposes, first and foremost.
If you are having a medical emergency, or feel that you are a
danger to yourself or others, please call 911.
Asking for help is a sign of strength, not weakness.
A list of resources is available at the back of this book.

—Annie Lane

Annie Lane

Old Flame Brings Problems

DEAR ANNIE: I have been a widow for almost 10 years. I'm financially secure, socially active and attractive. My old high school sweetheart contacted me a few years after I lost my husband. After months of phone contact, he came to visit. I had asked whether he was married. He said no, that he'd been divorced for over 25 years. What he didn't mention was that he was in a 25-year committed relationship with a woman he financially supported and lived with. When I discovered this, he told me she would be moving out in the near future. That took two years! She did leave when she found out about me. I should have run far away at that time, but he assured me that he would never hurt me and that I should trust him.

Imagine my surprise to have my doctor tell me at my yearly exam that I have HPV. I was heartbroken, angry and afraid for my future health, as this often leads to cervical cancer. I immediately broke up with him. He was my first love and could be very charming. I miss him today, three months later. I would like to have a limited relationship with him as an old friend, but he has blocked my phone number and email address.

How do I keep from wanting to tell my story to friends? The woman or women he's with need to know about the health risk. Should I try to alert them to this or fade away?

—*Stupid Senior*

DEAR SENIOR: I refuse to call you stupid. No more beating yourself up. Please extend the same compassion to yourself that you would to a friend in this situation. I'm sorry this man added insult to injury by leaving you with health concerns in addition to cheating. That being said, are you sure he was the source of the virus? According to the National Cervical Cancer Coalition, "it can take weeks, months, or even years after exposure to HPV before symptoms develop or the virus is detected," and this usually makes it "impossible to determine when or from whom HPV may have been contracted." (Visit http://www.nccc-online.org for more information.)

I think it's perfectly fine and healthy for you to talk to friends about what you're going through, but do not do so to get revenge on him; rather, do it to help heal yourself emotionally.

Long-Distance Distrust

DEAR ANNIE: My girlfriend and I are in a long-distance relationship. We met in grad school. She finished up in the spring and got a job up north, about a 12-hour drive away, while I stayed behind to finish school. We decided that we would try to make a long-distance relationship work for this year and that then I would find a job near her.

A good buddy of mine happens to live in the same city as she does. Recently, he sent me a screenshot from a dating app that shows you other people in your area who are looking to hook up. It was my girlfriend. She had created a profile on the app and posted flirty photos. I recognized one of the photos from a beach trip we'd taken, but she had cropped me out of the picture. Her "About Me" section said, "New to the city! Looking for fun!"

I immediately called and confronted her. She acted surprised by my anger, saying she was just using that app to make friends. She got angry and said it hurt that I didn't trust her. By the time we got off the phone, I felt bad for doubting her. That night, I had a pizza delivered to her place as an apology.

But now I'm having second thoughts. Am I being paranoid?

—*Wondering*

DEAR WONDERING: You should have sent that pizza to your buddy. He saved you a lot of trouble and an expensive move for a woman who clearly doesn't think much of you—first cheating on you and then disrespecting your intelligence with a whopper like that. Time to crop her out of the picture as she's already done to you.

Cold Shoulder After Divorce

DEAR ANNIE: I recently went on vacation with my mom, stepdad and siblings. We went to the river where my stepdad has been going for about 30 years. Everyone else in the community has been going there every year for just as long, if not longer. Now, my mom and stepdad met each other while they were married, and, well, you can put the rest together. Many families we know have taken sides ever since, so being the daughter, I'm no stranger to weird vibes in social situations and people choosing sides.

Upon meeting the rivergoers, I quickly realized that some of them were on my stepdad's ex-wife's side. How did I know? They avoided talking to us and didn't invite us to partake in group watersport activities. In one case, after I introduced myself, the woman looked at me, scoffed and walked away. There were plenty of nice people, though, so we still had a great time.

This isn't something I take personally. The situation has nothing to do with me, and the affair happened six years ago. If they're getting all hung up about something that's not even their business, that's their problem. But I never know whether I should stand up for myself, kill them with kindness or just ignore them. What do you think?

—*Boating With Baggage*

DEAR BOATING: It sounds as if you're expert at navigating these treacherous rapids, so kudos. It's incredibly mature of you not to take the antics of your stepdad's ex-wife's friends personally. The bitterness and resentment they're holding on to is only dragging them down.

Continue being pleasant in the face of their ugly attitudes. Pretend you're oblivious to their bad vibes. They can scoff until they're blue in the face. But don't be a doormat, either. If one of them says something outright rude to you, you have a right to stand up for yourself.

All Not in the Family

DEAR ANNIE: My husband of two years was divorced from his ex six years ago. They had no children. The divorce was the result of infidelity on his part. When we began to date, he was very upfront with me about his dysfunctional marriage and about how his infidelity was the result of his being shut down by his wife in the bedroom for several years. They split, and she bought a house 1 mile away from him. He was honest about what happened and was very clear he had nothing to hide.

She has suddenly become all about "the family." It is as if she is taking out her anger over the divorce on me. 1) I wasn't the girl he was seeing back then. 2) It isn't her business.

Now it has been made perfectly clear that his family recognizes her as family and not me, and he is also treated like an outcast. She is front and center of everything, attending all family events.

I have tried to be nice and civil to her, but she is always rude to me. My husband's sister finally came around and apologized, recognizing that the ex's being around all the time does pose a problem.

I love him, and I hate to see him hurting like this. How should I handle his family when we both feel like outcasts?

—*Outcast*

DEAR OUTCAST: Though you can't control other people's actions, you can control your reactions to other people. Try to be sympathetic to your husband's ex-wife. Clearly, she has struggled to move on from their marriage. By focusing all of her energy on his family, she is wasting opportunities to meet a new partner and move on with her life. As far as how your in-laws are treating your husband and you, all you can do is lend your support and love to him.

It sounds as if you're off to a good start toward repairing your relationship and, in turn, your husband's relationship with his family, given his sister extended an olive branch and apologized. Try as best you can to be the bigger person and accept her apology. Let go of any resentment you hold. Let's hope that in the future, he will once again feel close to his family. As is always the case, communication is key. When your feelings and expectations are clear—and you are clear on everybody else's—then the situation will go more smoothly.

Hidden Conversation

DEAR ANNIE: Today I asked my husband whether he had heard from anyone over the holidays, just thinking that maybe one of our friends had contacted him instead of me. He looked right into my eyes and said, "No." Something about the way he answered caused me to do something I had never done before: I checked his email when he left to go shopping. Sure enough, he had heard from someone, and I now discover he has been emailing with this person (a woman) for some time.

Knowing he is having a running conversation with another woman—plus the fact that he lied about it—has me wondering what to do. He's been a liar in the past, but I thought he had moved beyond that. We've broken up before, but we worked things out and got back together. I trusted in him to do the right thing this time around, and until today, I believed everything was fine.

Of course, the other side of this is that I wouldn't have even known this if I hadn't gone into his email. Right now, I am brooding over it and letting the anger build up inside me. Should I admit I snooped and I know about his lies, or should I just keep quiet and start the process of ending the relationship? Honesty is important to me. But then, I was dishonest by snooping. Help!

—*Liar, Liar*

DEAR LIAR, LIAR: Come clean to your husband about your snooping, and in that same conversation, ask him to go to marriage counseling. By the time you find yourself wanting to snoop on your partner, mistrust has been festering for quite some time. It seems neither of you has been able to shake past issues. So perhaps this recent incident will turn out to be a very good thing for your marriage in the long run, if it persuades you both to truly open up to each other and begin the process of rebuilding trust from the ground up.

Writing Down What's Hard to Say Aloud

DEAR ANNIE: I am trying to decide if I should print out the following letter and give it to my wife. What do you think?

Dear Leigh:

My goal here is not to blame or accuse or criticize. I just want to find a way to better communicate. Please don't get angry or frustrated or feel like I am trying to attack you because that is not the case.

The area I am writing about today is intimate relations. We have talked about them before and I've really tried to provide the requested time, space and distance since last summer. Unfortunately, I've not seen any real improvements in this area. My purpose is not to criticize or cast blame or anything more than to clear the air and understand needs and expectations. We have virtually no sex life. I have been the "initiator" in every encounter over the last few months. In the past year, you've had three, possibly four overnight sleepovers at the homes of various female friends, leaving your husband and small child at home.

My bottom line is that I feel like we are roommates who sleep in the same bed and raise a child together. We seem to live our own lives other than that. My weight gain hasn't helped, and I know that, too.

At any rate, regardless of what the answers are, I really need you to be clear and honest with me, with respect to whether you have ever fulfilled your physical needs elsewhere since we got married 14 years ago, or even if you wanted to but didn't follow through. Have you been thinking about it? If so, and you've yet to take action, is this something you want to explore? These questions keep me up at night. We need to talk about these things, no matter what the answers are.

—Mitch

DEAR MITCH: While it's important to have eye-to-eye heart-to-hearts with your spouse, letters can be a great way to broach sensitive subjects that might otherwise arouse defensiveness. The format gives each partner space to organize and communicate his or her thoughts and feelings. So, yes, give your wife this letter, along with a day to herself to read, absorb and articulate a response.

That said, this is but one tool. A marriage counselor could equip you with a full kit for rebuilding the channels of communication and repairing the foundation of your marriage. I encourage you to ask your wife to attend. Please let me know how it goes.

Shark on the Hunt

DEAR ANNIE: My husband has a friend, "Ralph," who is half his age and was recently married. Ralph's wife, "Katherine," is always texting my husband, and not me, to make plans to go out to eat. I have asked my husband several times to text Ralph back instead of his wife, but he has not. When we go out to eat, Ralph's wife always wants to sample my husband's food and taste his drink; she never samples mine. She never asks if she can taste test. She just does it. She also likes to sit beside my husband.

The other night, she stood at the bar talking to both of us with her arm on the back of my husband's chair and not mine. One time, I got back to the table just in time to hear her say that she wouldn't be getting any love from Ralph tonight. My husband replied that he wouldn't be getting any from me either. That's because my husband falls asleep as soon as he gets home. Her reply was that my husband should leave with her and I should leave with Ralph.

She once told me that she and a girlfriend had read that they could make $7,000 a month if they worked for a sugar daddy. She has been married 10 months and is already complaining about Ralph. I see no love between them when they are together. My husband feels that his relationship with her is more like a father/daughter relationship and does not see anything wrong with it. My husband tells me nothing would ever happen between them and it's all in my head. I think she is looking for a sugar daddy. What are your thoughts?

—*Am I Right to Be Suspicious?*

DEAR SUSPICIOUS: Trust your instincts on this one. She sounds like a shark circling your marriage. Picking food off your husband's plate, texting him instead of you and placing her arm on the back of your husband's chair are all signs that she is going in for the kill. The question is how to put an end to this shark and not allow your marriage to be swallowed up by her.

Don't continue to be put in a situation where you are accusing and complaining about her while your husband rushes to her defense. Instead, trust your instincts and insist that the friendship ends. The alternative is that she continues to drive a wedge through your marriage, and that is not OK. You and your husband should be a unified front protecting your marriage from circling predators.

Gossip Leads to Nothing Good

DEAR ANNIE: My co-worker, "Jane," is the front-desk person and has a bird's-eye view to everything. For the past several years she has noticed that it appears that my supervisor is having an affair with another co-worker. I, too, have noticed what appear to be signs of an affair. Although I do not approve (if this is the case), I am able to work without it disturbing me. Recently, it has started to affect my co-worker so much that she is now saying that this a hostile work environment.

My question is this, should I mention something to my supervisor before my co-worker takes it to HR? She has threatened to do this, but she is the type who is normally all talk no action.

I feel uncomfortable saying something to my supervisor, but if it got as far as HR then I would feel disloyal for not having given him a warning. I don't know how to handle this sensitive situation.

—Awkwardness at the Office

DEAR AWKWARDNESS: First, stop chatting with Jane about the alleged affair. Speculation without action amounts to gossip, and nothing good can come of it. The next time she tries to talk to you about it, tell her you're uncomfortable discussing it, and change the subject.

Of course, she's free to go to HR about the issue. And if it's impacting her ability to do her job, then she definitely should. Do not intercede: What would the endgame be in telling your boss? It would make Jane vulnerable to preemptive attacks, and it would insulate your boss from the consequences of his own bad decisions. If he is having an inappropriate affair, that's a bad bet he chose to wager. Let the chips fall where they may; the stakes aren't yours.

Annie Lane

Keep the Fun of Fantasy Alive

DEAR ANNIE: You answer a lot of questions about infidelity, jealousy and therapy. This is a different way to look at it: Sex is 80 percent fantasy and 20 percent physical. The physical part is the same whoever your partner is. It's the fantasy part that creates the excitement. That's how they sell magazines and love stories. No one buys Playboy for the news articles.

Remember the excitement and fantasy of your honeymoon? It might have gotten a little routine and unexciting over the years. The key is to recreate the fantasies for your partner. Then you can make love to anyone in the world and never leave home. Just have fun. It's cheaper than therapy, and it stops the arguing and complaining about each other.

—Happy

DEAR HAPPY: Thank you for your amusing and insightful letter. I love the idea of looking at what you can create with your partner and having happiness and excitement as goals.

Wrecking a Home and a Career Opportunity

DEAR ANNIE: Recently, I met "Todd" through a friend of a friend. I went back to school to study graphic design a couple years ago and will be graduating this fall. Todd is also a graphic designer, so our mutual friend introduced us so that Todd could give me career advice and maybe even get me a job or apprenticeship at the company where he works.

When I met Todd, instantly, sparks flew. We met at a coffee shop and it was only supposed to be a half-hour chat about graphic design, but we ended up talking for more than two hours about our favorite artists, our backgrounds—pretty much everything. He has the most beautiful eyes and made a lot of prolonged eye contact as we talked. Though it was supposed to just be a professional advice-giving session, it felt to me more like a first date.

I really want to pursue something with Todd, but the only problem is he's married. I met his wife, "Margaret," a few weeks ago at our mutual friend's (the one who introduced us) birthday party. Margaret was very frosty toward me. She does not seem nearly as fun as me; she was really just a dour person. She's also about 10 years older than me and not as pretty. (I'm 32 and have never had trouble getting attention from men.)

I can tell Todd and I have chemistry and just get the feeling that he'd rather be spending time with me than his plain wife. He's invited me to a mixer with graphic design industry folks to ostensibly "help my career," but I know that's just a guise. I want to make a move after we leave. I talked to a friend about this and she told me that homewrecking is a sin. Well, in my view, you can't wreck a home that isn't already on shaky ground. If Todd strays with me, I won't be the cause of their breakup. I'll just be the straw that broke the camel's back. Do you agree?

For what it's worth, they don't have any kids and have only been married a few years.

—*Ready to Pounce*

DEAR READY TO POUNCE: Keep your paws to yourself. Yes, good relationships should be able to withstand adversity, but that doesn't mean it's your job to deliberately dole it out. On top of that, I think you're setting yourself up for embarrassment. "Prolonged eye contact" is a thing that people sometimes do in conversation. Todd's only interactions with you so far have been in the context of career help—help you'll lose if you lust after him.

Limit your communication with Todd to strictly professional inquiries, and if you can't manage that, then discontinue contact altogether. Lastly, take a good long look in the mirror and do some serious reflecting, because your comments about his wife's appearance only make you look ugly.

Moving Out and Moving On

DEAR ANNIE: I lived with my husband for 50 years. We met spontaneously, and I moved in with him soon afterward. He was different from the norm. He was smart, always outgoing and had many great friends. I fell deeply in love. We got married after a few years together and began to build our careers in businesses, where we both became respected and successful in our fields. Over those years, we also partied excessively, and hung out with people who would eventually end up in prison. We moved beyond our youthful acts and raised a family. But he never stopped bragging about his earlier, danger-filled exploits to anyone and everyone. And his stories have grown to new exaggerated versions or downright lies.

I also painfully discovered that he considers himself a ladies' man, and has been secretly wining and dining other women. As much as I worked to make our lives better and make myself more attractive, I became more and more depressed. I felt I wasn't good enough. I confronted him several times about all of these issues and nothing ever improved.

Through an "aha" moment and research, I came to discover that I married a sociopath. I have been trying to fix someone who cannot be fixed. He ignores my attempts to improve our relationship because he doesn't care. He's not wired for it. I am finally working through all of this through therapy, particularly mindfulness meditation. I feel like a new person. I'm writing this because the symptoms have been there all along, and I was too busy, tired or ashamed to deal with it until now. I wish more information had been available to me earlier in my life about the prospects for a loving relationship with a sociopath. I found that he may often say and do the right things, but it is all an act and short-lived. With no regrets, I am now moving on with the second half of my time on this earth! I am happier and really enjoy life.

—*Breathing Free*

DEAR BREATHING: And I am so happy for you. I appreciate your sharing your story here so that it might be a light for someone who's in the dark, as you were.

Half-Truths Cause Heartbreak

DEAR ANNIE: My husband constantly lies by omission of details of what he has done.

He has had two affairs with other women—that I know of. He thinks if he tells part of the truth, it is OK. That is how his mind works, and he doesn't care what I think.

What is wrong with him? His mother was the same way.

—Questioning in PA

DEAR QUESTIONING: No matter what sort of mental gymnastics your husband engages in to convince himself he's not a bad guy, a half-told truth is a lie. If he wants to make things right, he'll agree to go to marriage counseling with you. A counselor might help uncover whatever deep-seated issues drive him toward cheating and lying, and there you two can work together to build a new foundation, because his past actions have put a rot in the old one. Taking things apart and building your relationship anew is your best hope at having a healthy married life.

Brother Is a Doormat

DEAR ANNIE: My brother is married to a woman who is having an affair. They both are on their second marriage and have three kids together. The woman has two other children. The problem is that this woman has given up all rights to her first two children. She did this for financial reasons, but it backfired because the court ordered her to pay child support.

She then became pregnant with twins and stopped working. She did nothing but lie on the couch all day. She thinks it is OK to be married to one man and to have another younger man, who is a little slow, on the side. This man is at her every beck and call. He will spend all his money on her and lose everything he has.

But my brother is so dumb and stupid; he is letting this go on so there will be no fighting. On weekends, she feels like she does not need to be a mother. She did have to get a job to pay back child support for her first two children or go to jail. She only works part time, while her husband works full time. Despite this, he does all the cooking. She won't cook for the kids or anyone else. On weekends, she will leave her husband (my brother) and go to stay at the other man's place so he can spend his money on her. This is not good for kids. How do we convince my brother he is better off without her, or get them some help?

—*Concerned Sister*

DEAR CONCERNED SISTER: Watching your brother and your nieces and nephews be neglected as their mother has an affair is sad for everyone involved. While you can't "force" your brother to leave her, you can provide emotional support for your brother and his children. Remember that "love" can be blind, and right now it sounds like your brother does not want to take off the blindfold.

Try to build up your brother's self-esteem so that he will eventually have the courage to leave her or stand up for himself and not be treated like a doormat.

Cheating Pig

DEAR ANNIE: My friend has been dating the same guy for about a year, and I have always gotten along with him just fine. He has become my friend, too. I've always thought they seem so happy together, and it makes me glad to see my friend treated well by someone she cares about. Friendship is everything to me. That's why I'm struggling now. Another friend of mine, from a completely different circle of friends, was telling me about the guy she recently hooked up with. Well, lo and behold, he's already taken ... by my other friend. I'm really struggling with this information and feeling conflicted. First of all, I can't believe that this guy had me fooled while he's been fooling around with two of my friends. But I just don't know whom to confront first and how to get this pig out of my friends' lives!

—Fierce Friend

DEAR FIERCE: "Pig" is too kind a word. But I digress.

You need to talk to both of your friends. (Let's count it as some shred of a silver lining that the two of them aren't friends with each other.)

First, talk to the one whom he cheated with. Don't be accusatory. Start with "I'm sure you weren't aware of this, but ... " Don't get into too many details with her. Keep the conversation short and sweet.

Then comes the hard part. You need to tell your friend her boyfriend cheated. Do it soon—like, now. The longer you put off news such as this the harder it is to share. Put forth your comfiest shoulder to cry on, and tell her, as gently as possible, that he cheated. It's not going to be fun. You'll be in for a long few weeks as a human sounding board. But in the end, your friend will move on.

As for that pig? He'll go "wah, wah, wah" all the way home.

Picture Causing Worry

DEAR ANNIE: Recently, I got married after being single and a widow for 23 years. My husband and I are in our late 70s and very active. We went on a tour to the Midwest. There was a very attractive 70-plus woman with whom I noticed my husband flirting, and she with him. I mentioned that I did not appreciate the attention he was throwing her way, and he assured me it was all in fun.

He later needed help with the photos on his phone. As I was helping him, there was a picture of her and her alone. Not in a group. I questioned him as to why he had a picture of her in his phone, and his response was that he didn't know how it got there. He said it must have been a mistake.

He has assured me that he loves me and is not interested in anyone else. I can't seem to get this out of my head. I have prayed on this but to no avail. I thank you in advance for any advice you have on how to handle this situation. I cannot let it go.

—Worried About Wandering Eyes

DEAR WORRIED: It is understandable that you would question why your husband had a single picture of the woman that you thought he was flirting with. Expressing your jealousy is OK if done in a productive and matter-of-fact way. If you allow your jealousy to fester, it will only torment you. As William Penn said: "The jealous are troublesome to others but a torment to themselves."

You have a choice in regards to the picture: You can choose to believe him—that it just got there—or you can call him out. And perhaps you don't mind if he looks or even flirts a little with another woman, but it's the lying that really bothers you. Looking and not touching, or even flirting a little, with someone might be acceptable, but lying about it is a much bigger problem. It is the coverup that creates the most problems. Your husband would be much better served if he just said sorry for taking her picture and reassured you that he only has eyes for you.

Annie Lane

DNA Results Bombshell

DEAR ANNIE: Recently, I was contacted by a person who had just received results from a popular online DNA test, which I had also taken some time ago. She asked who I was. We share a great deal of DNA, so, naturally, she assumed that she would know me. Well, after looking through our shared DNA matches and carrying out some additional research, I realized that I do know her. We lived next door to each other when we were very young, and played together nearly every day.

Our DNA clearly demonstrates that we are half-siblings sharing the same father—my dad, who was married to my mother at the time. While I'm thrilled that we've found each other after more than 50 years, we are both a bit shocked at the realization that things are not at all what they seemed, for either of us. She was not expecting these results, and she had simply been seeking information on the family of the man she had always believed to be her father.

I'm really on the fence as to whether I should tell my two brothers about this. One was very close to dad, and the other had a more troubled relationship with him. Regardless of our love and respect for our father, this information would undoubtedly flavor their feelings. Mom and Dad are gone. There is no one left who could answer the many questions this brings up. My friend did not contact me looking for a new family, and has not expressed interest in meeting her other half-siblings. On the other hand, this information belongs to them as much as it belongs to me.

I feel that it would be wrong to hide this but am not sure it would serve any positive purpose, and might well affect my brothers' memories of Dad negatively. Should I tell my brothers we have a half-sister, the result of a relationship outside of our parents' marriage? Will this accomplish anything other than bringing up questions that can no longer be answered?

—Suddenly a Sister

DEAR SUDDENLY A SISTER: When it comes to questions this complicated, there are no right or wrong answers. But I'd lean toward sharing the news with your brothers, if only because they are your closest living family members and secrets build walls. Whichever you decide, I'd love to hear from you in the future about how it went.

Not-So-Sunny Marriage

DEAR ANNIE: I'm a 30-year-old male in my first year of marriage to a charming, beautiful woman, "Sonny." I am madly in love with this woman, and she says the same to me. This is a second marriage for both of us.

Unfortunately, I'm finding out that she has lied to me about a number of things, and my love for her is being weakened by these revelations. We met shortly after she had broken up with another man. She told me that it was over. However, during our dating prior to marriage I learned that she was still seeing him, and sleeping with him on nights we were not together. At one point, she even suggested that we three should live together, and she would alternate nights with each of us. I wasn't about to accept that. We're married now, but I know she still has at least a phone relationship with him.

Her mother has recently moved in with us because I was told that circumstances in her life created that need. I've since learned that those dire straits were untrue. Most nights I go to bed alone because Sonny is chatting with her mother, with whom she's always had a close relationship, and with whom she lived when we first met.

Recently, Sonny has contacted a man she met during her first marriage. She set up a meeting with him. I have no idea what transpired between them, neither initially nor at this time. I do know he has a child named for her.

I've just learned that one of her children, supposedly from her first marriage, was fathered by another man during a period of separation in that marriage.

On a recent romantic long weekend to a tropical destination, Sonny wanted no part of any sexual romance. Of course, this crushed me. Though I always think of "Sonny" as an enthusiastic sexual partner, she never initiates intimacy between us.

We have been to a marriage counselor, whose concluding comment to me was, "Some beautiful women are like that," meaning they need attention from other men, I think. I'm seriously considering divorce, though I'm still in love with her. I'm feeling used, and find myself responding to some situations between us with anger. Can this marriage be saved?

—*Feeling Torn*

DEAR TORN: You are not painting a very sunny picture of Sonny. Unless the two of you had a previous understanding that infidelity was part of the deal, her actions would leave anyone feeling used. Your therapist's observation that "some beautiful women are just this way" seems dismissive and flippant. You might consider seeing another therapist.

Unless you are OK with Sonny's infidelity, this marriage will only bring you darkness and hurt. It's time to find a new therapist who helps you better understand what you would like out of a marriage.

And then you need to tell Sonny in no uncertain terms what that is, perhaps being faithful. And what's with her mother? Is she enabling or encouraging Sonny to split the two of you apart?

When I read your letter, I couldn't help but wonder why you married her if you knew she was cheating on you when you were dating. With good therapy, you can both decide if you want to stay together and make it work, or go your separate ways. Best of luck to you.

Still Hurting After Divorce

DEAR ANNIE: After 46 years, my husband decided to leave me soon after he met a gold-digger overseas.

He went about it in a cowardly manner, looking for his condo in secret, although his friends were in on his plans. I was devastated when I accidentally found out and confronted him about it. He admitted that he wanted to leave, and, soon after, did so.

For some time, I believed it was a late midlife crisis and he would soon come to his senses. But after several years of living apart, he demanded a divorce and I reluctantly agreed.

Soon after the divorce, he asked to become friends with me. I could not see having a friendship with someone who had treated me with such a lack of consideration and for whom I still feel anger and resentment. I am afraid that I will never have closure on this because he has not acknowledged how much he hurt me or how badly he treated me.

There is some satisfaction in rejecting his offer of friendship. I hope he has a twinge of regret for what he cast aside so cavalierly. Am I being unreasonable or vengeful in your opinion?

—Hurt and Angry

DEAR HURT AND ANGRY: No, you are not being unreasonable. In fact, you don't have to worry about how you are acting toward your ex-husband right now. Your life has been turned upside-down, and he is the one who caused it. Seek out a good therapist or counselor to work through some of your anger and frustration. Do things that make you happy. Don't worry about what he is thinking or doing. This is your chance to focus on you and to think about how you can heal and come out a stronger person.

It is understandable that, when we are hurt, it feels good to reject or wound the one who hurt us. Don't judge those feelings negatively. Just acknowledge them for now and know that eventually you will find forgiveness—not for him but for yourself. Then you can move on. But don't rush the process. Best of luck to you.

35-Year-Old Surprise

DEAR ANNIE: We received a shocking message on our answering machine a few days ago. A woman called and identified herself as a possible daughter from an affair 35 years ago. Later, a woman left a message saying she was the mother. I have not been in contact with this woman for 31 years!

Later, I told my wife of 30 years, to whom I have been faithful. When I made those vows, I meant every word of them.

But I felt that I should call the daughter back, as I respect the courage it took for her to call a total stranger and request that I take a DNA test with her.

My wife blew up! She said I have betrayed and disrespected her, and grievously wounded her for wanting to contact the "daughter." She said we would be getting a divorce and that she is out of here!

I have been thinking about all this and am wondering if someone is trying to break up our marriage. If I had a child with the "mother," why did she not tell me 35 years ago? Or some time before we parted ways?

We are both blindsided by this, and I am lost by the prospect of losing my wife and partner of 30 years.

—Lost and Confused

DEAR LOST AND CONFUSED: If you have truly been faithful to your wife for 30 years, and this is a daughter from your past, then, while it might be a large and difficult pill to swallow, your wife should support you. Continue an open dialogue with her about your feelings regarding this matter. You had a life before you met your wife, and this might be part of that previous life. Remind your wife that this does nothing to change the last 30 years you've had together. In good times and in bad, you have stuck with each other.

On the other hand, if someone is trying to break up your marriage, shame on them. The most important thing here is that you and your wife are a united front.

You also can't blame this woman for wanting to know who is her father. Perhaps now would be a good time to seek couples counseling.

Unforgiven Infidelity

DEAR ANNIE: Soldiers still cry 50 years after their experiences with horrendous trauma. The list goes on and on of the many things that people experience that they find very difficult to "get over." Most people are sensitive enough to realize which traumas are the ones that affect the suffering person for many, many years.

I'd like to add one trauma that I find gets zero sympathy from others—infidelity. My husband cheated on me when I was seven months pregnant with our second child. When he informed me about it, he added that he had "never loved me," and, when I asked, he said that yes, he "loved his mistress." This came as a complete shock to me. In fact, I shook so violently that I saw a doctor the next day, fearing that I might lose the baby, and I was put on tranquilizers. Once on them, I could barely care for my oldest child.

We parted for a while and, during that period of time, I felt as if he had died. In addition, I felt that he had gone out of his way to hurt me on purpose. My "best friend" never contacted me after finding out. My mother-in-law called me a "heathen." My parents eventually said they could help me but only for a while—not for any length of time. I had no one else to count on or even talk to.

At that point, I spent a night thinking about the gun kept in our closet and using it on myself to end my hopeless future. I reconsidered, after thinking about who would care for my older child. I absolutely did not want this mistress raising my baby. Yes, the mistress knew I was pregnant. There is much more ugliness to this story, but my point is that for more than 50 years I've suffered in silence. At my prompting, we tried to make a go of the marriage, but it has been a pretentious sham from that moment on.

Did I lose whatever love existed between us? Yes. I cry at weddings when people promise to love and be faithful for the rest of their lives. I cry at shows that bring back the memories.

Do I think my children appreciate what I felt I did for them? I told them when they were adults, and no, I don't think they realize the gravity of the situation at the time.

Therapists? The last one announced, "What needs to be done here is for you to forgive your husband." What about his learning to be ashamed and make things better with what he has said since?

Spouses of cheaters don't get any sympathy, help or chances to talk it out with friends. People seem to think this is one trauma that gets healed on its own.

—*Still Hurting*

DEAR STILL HURTING: I am very sorry that you suffered from emotionally shocking and painful distress. You are correct that infidelity, while you were pregnant and completely alone—combined with hearing that your husband loved his mistress and didn't love you—constitutes a trauma.

But I would suggest examining why your therapist advised, "What needs to be done here is for you to forgive your husband." It is not to get your husband off the hook for what he did to you, but to get yourself off the hook. Holding a grudge is hurting you more than anyone else. As Mark Twain wrote, "Anger is an acid that can do more harm to the vessel in which it is stored than to anything on which it is poured."

Theologian Lewis B. Smedes added, "To forgive is to set a prisoner free and to discover that the prisoner was you."

Annie Lane

Free from Expectations

DEAR ANNIE: To any woman who is in love with a married man, I want to share some very important advice: Don't go there. It only ends up with loneliness and heartbreak. You may think your situation is different. It is not. He may promise to leave his marriage, but he won't. Friends will tell you that at the time, but you won't heed their advice. When you raise your friends' concerns with your lover, he will explain that your friends are just jealous.

Really listen to him. He's very clever at playing with your emotions. Remember: If he cheats on his wife, he will cheat on you. And he did!

—*Older and Wiser*

DEAR OLDER: A resounding yes to this. I'm sorry that you had to learn this lesson the hard way. May someone reading this heed your advice and avoid the same pitfalls.

Rebuilding After Betrayal

DEAR ANNIE: I read "Dear Annie" now, just as I read "Ask Ann Landers" and "Dear Abby" starting in the 1950s. I hope you can give me some advice.

My husband, "Fred," and I have been married for 58 years. We met when we were both working in Washington, D.C. We were 18 years old. We dated for 3 1/2 years. He presented himself to be charming, a man of good morals, sweet, kind, a Christian and a virgin. I thought he loved me more than anyone. I had some reservations because he spoke of "Mother" frequently, often using the phrase

How Can I Forgive My Cheating Partner?

"Mother said."

Once I got to know him better, I felt he had matured. But after marriage, he began to have temper tantrums. I was shocked.

After losing our first baby to a miscarriage, Fred was drafted into the Army and soon sent to Korea. I had begged him to join the Guard, but at his mother's suggestion, he refused.

After he returned home, I became pregnant and had a little girl. A year and a half later, we had a son, born a couple of weeks prior to Christmas.

While out shopping around that time, I saw Fred using a pay phone, so I walked up behind him and overheard a romantic conversation. He made up a plausible lie, and I let it go. Years went by, and he was not good to me.

Last year, after 57 years of marriage, he decided to tell all. He now tells me he was calling a woman for a second date during the week of Christmas. He later called to see if the coast was clear, as she was married, too. He also told me he had slept with prostitutes while in Korea and then had relations with other women in D.C., Chicago—where we lived for a time—and then Memphis, where we now live. He claims he has always loved me and the encounters with other women were "just sex," as if that makes a difference to me.

I am devastated beyond belief.

We are now 80, and I have stage 4 cancer. People tell me I look as if I am in my 60s, and the cancer is in remission. Our children are grown. We have completed one year of counseling. He has been diagnosed as a "sex addict," and I have PTSD. Our lives are in ruin. He denies that he's addicted to sex, and he denies that it was caused by his domineering mother, as counselors have suggested.

I am uncertain as to what to do. I worked hard and invested well and can afford to support myself. Counseling helped some but not much. Right now, I am unable to make logical decisions. Do you have any words of wisdom for me?

—*A Lifelong Reader*

DEAR LIFELONG READER: You sound like a remarkable and very strong woman. My advice is that you make the decision NOT to make a decision at this time. Instead, focus on yourself and making you—and only you—happy, whatever that might mean. Go to your church, visit your children and grandchildren. While you're healing from this trauma of deception, it's perfectly reasonable to take a break from your husband. There are different types of therapy you could try. Continue with your counseling and perhaps add some meditation or prayer groups. Spend time with your friends.

At some point, you will realize that your husband had a very troubled upbringing, which contributed to his acting out. This does not excuse his behavior, but hopefully, the realization will give you some peace of mind. Remember that his actions had nothing to do with you or how much he loved you but rather with how little he loved himself.

Breaking the Cycle of Guilt and Pain

DEAR ANNIE: About two years ago, I was pregnant with my firstborn. About five months into the pregnancy, my partner, the father, cheated on me. When I found out about it, I was devastated; I didn't know what to do with myself.

I felt he did it to me on purpose with the reasoning of "getting even" because I'd cheated on him years before. It was one time, and I felt pushed away and insecure at the time. Of course, cheating didn't make me feel better; it made me feel worse.

His cheating on me while I was pregnant made me feel that I didn't mean anything to him. I felt stupid because it was someone we knew, someone I was hanging around thinking that nothing was going on between them. I've even hosted her at our house with a few other people even though they were messing around with each other during that time.

Now I feel back in the same place, and I don't know how to stop this running circle of guilt, like it was my fault he cheated on me. I really wish I could get over it and move on, because that's what I should do. But I have flashbacks and make up scenarios in my head. Please give me some advice. I'm tired of feeling this way. I need a way to let go of this heavy weight on my shoulders.

—Lost in Love

DEAR LOST IN LOVE: He needs to help you take that weight off your shoulders. It is possible to move past cheating in a relationship, but only with sincere remorse, a commitment to healing the wounds and a willingness to have trust restored. You both need to either work together toward those tenets or consider separating now and cultivating a respectful nonromantic relationship as co-parents for the long-term.

Don't Mess with Married Men

DEAR ANNIE: Regarding dating married men: I've been there. I was 22, and he was 37. He was very good-looking, had a great job, lived in the suburbs ... and had a terrible marriage. He saw me as the hippie—living the life that he missed. He and I would spend time together and take long walks, go for drinks, have a great physical relationship, etc. Then he would go home to his wife and kids, to the mortgage, the bills, etc. In other words, he would go home to real life!

I was his escape, his fantasy, his vacation. We didn't end up together—though his marriage eventually broke up because his wife found out about the revolving door of women in his life. If you think that you have a permanent relationship with a married man, then give him an ultimatum and a deadline. I guarantee you that he will find many reasons to not follow through. If he does follow through and you commit to forever, eventually *you* will be his middle-aged wife with the burdens of real life. Then, he will, again, need an escape. And there will be "the you that you were when he first found you" waiting to give him a shoulder to cry on.

—Been There, Done That

DEAR BEEN THERE: If your letter convinces even one person to stop waiting for him to leave his wife (or her to leave his husband), it will have done good work. Thanks for writing.

Struggling to Trust Again

DEAR ANNIE: About two years ago, my husband had a relationship with another woman. The only reason I found out was that she called my home and told me all the sordid details. He then admitted it was all true. My question to you now is: Should I trust him again or leave him?

—Tortured

DEAR TORTURED: Indeed, those are the options—because you cannot stay with him without trusting him. But you can't simply force yourself to trust him, either. You're going to need a lot of help to get to that point.

Talk to your husband about seeking out that help together through marriage counseling. Know that counseling doesn't have to be an indefinite, ongoing thing; even a few sessions can help equip you both with tools for repairing trust and rebuilding your relationship. By doing the work, you two can come out the other side with a stronger foundation than ever.

Confused Over Two-Timer

DEAR ANNIE: My former boyfriend has a wife in the Philippines. He used to sometimes say, "Oh, stay with me, and we can keep sleeping together even when she moves to this country." Why would someone say something like that? I have a difficult time figuring out what he really meant.

—Perplexed Ex

DEAR PERPLEXED: I have a harder time understanding why you stuck around long enough for him to say that more than once. Clearly, he has no respect for you or for his wife. But the most important word in your letter is "former." Thank goodness that he's no longer your boyfriend. Pity to that woman if she's still his wife.

Annie Lane

Infidelity in the Inbox

DEAR ANNIE: My husband and I have been married for more than 50 years. We have had a great life together, sharing a lot of the same interests.

We had a great friendship with another couple. Several years ago, the husband caught my husband and his wife sexting each other. I do believe it was a one-time thing, as she was drinking and the circumstances pointed to being a one-night thing. I wanted to forgive and forget, as she was a really great friend. However, her husband insisted that we have no further contact with each other.

We have another friend who is a single mom with two grown children. They live a couple of hundred miles from us. For some reason, she started texting my husband about issues she has had with her children. Over the years, they have continued to text each other, but it is getting more and more frequent. One time I looked at his text messages, and she was sending him pictures of herself. She is beautiful and younger. I told him that I was not comfortable with all the texting and the pictures she sends. Since then, I have found them texting a lot more. I confronted her, and she said that my husband is her best friend and a big support system to her. She has a lot of issues with her grown children. I told my husband that I did not have an issue with their friendship, but my issue is his keeping it from me.

I asked that he tell me about her texting, and what's going on. He agreed. But nothing has changed. I knew they were still texting, and he wasn't saying anything to me, so I tried to check his messages from his computer, but he changed the password. When I asked him what his new password was, he gave me a number, but when I have tried it, it doesn't work. So I have gone behind his back and checked his messages on his phone and have found that they pretty much text daily. He has not said a word to me about it. And I have noticed at times that he deletes her messages but not anyone else's, so I am feeling he is trying to hide them from me. I have yet to confront him with this. Am I being stupid about this or should I be concerned? His lying is what bothers me about this whole situation.

—Disgruntled Wife

DEAR DISGRUNTLED WIFE: The first time you caught your husband sexting another woman should have called for some serious relationship repairs. Not just sweeping it under the rug as a one-time thing. That behavior is unacceptable, and if you're going to stay married to him, then some serious counseling should be done.

Fool me once, shame on you; fool me twice, shame on me. Your husband is lying to you and keeping secrets about his correspondence with another woman. Kindly tell this woman that she needs to find a professional therapist to help her with her grown children problems, and she needs to stay away from your husband.

Your husband has lied to you many times, and his behavior points to him knowing better. Otherwise, he wouldn't feel the need to delete these messages. It is not unreasonable for you to ask him for honesty and openness in his communication. It is time to go into marriage counseling and have your husband come clean. You sound like too kind of a woman to be lied to and taken for granted. It is time to stick up for yourself and tell him no more, once and for all.

Annie Lane

Sex Addiction Secret

DEAR ANNIE: When I was married, it was an unhappy one. Instead of counseling, I had a total of 14 different affairs within a few years. I got help from therapy for sex and love addicts. I understood where I went wrong.

Now, I'm dating one guy. The other day, when we were watching TV, he said that "sex addict" is a made-up term. I didn't say anything because I never told him that part of my past. Should I tell him? I think people would look down on me, so I've never told anyone.

I know he would look at me differently, and probably he'll think that I would cheat on him. So far, I have made it sound like I haven't been with a lot of men. I'm 55, by the way. Sex love addiction is real, and therapy did help me. Should I still keep it a secret?

—*Too Much Info?*

DEAR TOO MUCH INFO: We are only as sick as our secrets. You are in recovery and have received treatment for your addiction. Tell your boyfriend about your past. If he is really the one for you, then he will love and accept you, blemishes and all. Vulnerability can be contagious. Now that your relationship is opening up, be prepared for him to reveal some skeletons in his closet, too.

If you are still in touch with your therapist, you might benefit by bringing your boyfriend to a session, so you and your therapist can paint a more complete picture of what happened and how you have changed. Vulnerability and honesty are pillars to eventually building the house you would like to have in an honest and loving marriage.

Back-to-Back Betrayal

DEAR ANNIE: My husband and I have been together for 30 years and are in our 50s. About five years ago, our friends' daughter, "Michelle," started hanging out at our house. She is about 30 years old.

Out of nowhere, my husband decided that he wanted to help her by giving her a job with his construction company. He asked me what I thought, and I said no. He said that he wouldn't give her a job since I didn't approve.

Well, he went behind my back and hired her anyway and kept it a secret. I found out because she called the house wanting to know why he was late for work. We had major fights, especially after I found out that he was seeing her after work. He said no sex was involved.

Finally, I got her out of our lives, but I cannot get over his betrayal and the way he lied to me so he could see her. After that, I found him on online dating sites. I left him for two months, and he begged me to come home. I did. But I cannot forgive or forget. It eats at me every day. What should I do?

—*Betrayed*

DEAR BETRAYED: Michelle didn't cause your marriage's trust issues—those already existed, or you wouldn't have tried to forbid him from hiring her—and her apparent departure doesn't resolve them. No, that will require hard work on both your parts.

I encourage you to seek marriage counseling today: Perhaps it's possible for couples to work past cheating without it; it's also possible to scale a cliff face with only your bare hands. Why take that risk when there are perfectly good tools available?

If either of you refuses to try at least a few sessions, it could well be a dead-end. A marriage without trust is misery. And our days are too precious to give over to anger and bitterness.

Past Stuck in Future

DEAR ANNIE: Why am I in a quandary? Because I have been married most of my adult life, and I feel almost nothing for my partner of 33 years, and I'm sure we are both just going through the motions of the relationship. Don't misunderstand; I care deeply for this person. I just feel unfulfilled, and I can't explain it.

I guess it's complacency on both our parts. She says she loves me, but she had an affair a couple of years ago with her old boyfriend, and even with counseling, I can't seem to put it in the past.

Do you have any suggestions for me? Believe me, I have not been a saint in our marriage, but I have not cheated.

—*In a Quandary*

DEAR IN A QUANDRY: Your quandary is within you, and you have the choice of whether or not to truly forgive your wife. It sounds like you are—understandably—still feeling upset and hurt about her affair. Consider going back into counseling and working through your relationship. As far as feeling unfulfilled by her, fulfillment does not come from another person. It comes from within yourself. Healthy relationships flourish when two fulfilled people come together and accompany each other on this beautiful journey of life.

Porn Causing Divide in Marriage

DEAR ANNIE: My concern is my husband of 15 years. After we got married, I caught him looking at porn. When I confronted him, he told me he would stop. I believed him. About a month ago, I had a suspicion and confronted him, and he admitted that he had been looking again.

We have had our ups and downs, but this is something that just makes me sick. I am so hurt and just feel so belittled by his need for this. It has taken an emotional toll on me, and I need some advice. The past 10 years have been difficult for me healthwise, and the stress that this has put on me really worries me. I don't know whether I can forgive him and move on. I have always had issues with my self-esteem, and this just drives me to think I am not worth much. He says it means nothing to him. I see it as cheating, like if he had had an affair.

—*Stressed in PA*

DEAR STRESSED IN PA: Your husband's predilection for pornography is no reflection on you. You could be Aphrodite incarnate, and he'd still be looking at the stuff. This is his issue.

That said, the solution won't come from pointing fingers. You must approach your husband with empathy, not as an enemy. Ask him how he feels about his viewing porn; then explain how it makes you feel. Discuss what might help him drop this habit for good. Create an open dialogue and refuse to let anything be taboo between you two. Consider going to marriage counseling for help navigating these sensitive issues.

Lastly, I'd strongly encourage you to attend therapy on your own.

You said that you've always had low self-esteem: That won't magically change the day your husband stops looking at porn. A therapist can help you get to the root of those issues and weed them out, so you can grow and thrive in love and life in general.

Best to Leave It Alone

DEAR ANNIE: I have a cousin who is married, and he and his wife are very close to my wife and me. We started spending time together, not because of my cousin and me but because our wives hit it off and developed a close friendship. We spend the holidays together, visit one another at least once a week and go out together.

My cousin has two young daughters, one with his wife and another with his ex (who cheated on him, by the way), and he brings them along with us to spend the day together. Lately, my wife and I have been noticing that my cousin's wife has changed dramatically. She used to be more lively, talkative and happy, but now she seems distant and quiet, and sometimes she comes up with excuses to not go out with us. We think this change came about because we found out a couple of months ago (through my wife) that she is cheating on him.

She is employed at a correctional facility, and apparently, her lover is also employed there. We think that she suspects we know something about her infidelity, and that she might be trying to avoid us. My wife was able to obtain proof of this infidelity, and we don't know how to proceed.

Should we confront her about this? As I said, we are close, and it hurts me to see that she is doing this to my cousin, who has already gone through a situation like this. I see his wife going about her business with us and the rest of my family as if nothing has happened, and it makes me uncomfortable. She *knows* that her husband's ex cheated on him, and she accepted his daughter as her own.

My cousin was deeply hurt after he found out about his ex's cheating, and he has told us repeatedly that he will not tolerate another infidelity. He has tried to hurt himself on a couple of occasions. I am worried that if he finds out from someone else, he might try to hurt his wife or himself, or if he finds out that we knew about it all along and didn't tell him anything, then he might get upset with us and not want anything to do with us. I don't want this situation to escalate into something worse and know that I could have done something to stop it. What should I do?

—*Cousin Clueless*

DEAR COUSIN CLUELESS: Sit this one out. Mind your own business. It is always hard to see people you love in trouble, but sometimes the best thing you can do is send them kind thoughts and hope that things will work out or they will reach out to you. If he does, you can be an empathetic friend and tell him how much you support and love him.

Be Safe; Get Tested

DEAR ANNIE: In a future column, please stress that when someone is cheating (or being cheated on), they should be tested, along with everyone else involved—and the sooner the better.

—JP

DEAR JP: Great advice. I hope this isn't a lesson that you had to learn the hard way. Being cheated on is bad enough.

Readers can visit gettested.cdc.gov to find nearby facilities that will conduct testing free of charge.

Dousing Old Flames

DEAR ANNIE: In 1966, "Linda" and I met at church one night. I was "head over heels" in love with her immediately, and I believed then that she was, too. We were in our early 20s. I was in officer candidate school at the time. I gave her an engagement ring after we dated for a few months. I thought all was well. But a month or so later, she returned it. I think her mother nixed the wedding plans. I always suspected I wasn't a strong enough Baptist for her family.

Even though the engagement was off, we continued to see each other. I had a permanent change of station to Vietnam. While I was there, she sent me a "Dear John" letter, saying that she'd always love me as a person but she'd met someone else and they were engaged. I was devastated.

When I returned from Vietnam, I ended up meeting my wife. We started a family. Fifteen years later, after my father died, I got a condolence phone call from Linda, and we've kept up a correspondence ever since then, with phone calls and emails. To this day, I answer her emails, even though I sometimes wait a month or two to write back.

How Can I Forgive My Cheating Partner?

My dilemma is that I believe it wrong to be exchanging mail with an old flame. My wife is aware that we keep in touch and that we used to be an item, but she dismisses it as no threat. She thinks it's common enough to catch up now and then with old romantic partners, especially when a few decades have gone by. Still, I erase Linda's emails every time, as though I've something to hide.

One part of me says: "Wake up! She threw you under the bus. Get over it like millions of others." The other part hangs on to the illusion of love, of being in love—which is a sweet memory, don't you think? Hardly a day goes by that certain things don't remind me of this past. And she has said the same. Sometimes, it is anger and resentment of being rejected and feeling that I wasn't good enough, and other times it is of that broken-hearted feeling of how much I loved her.

I get along just fine with my current wife, but the memories of the past passion from 50 years ago are always lingering under the surface. I wish Linda would end it and set me free. Or I wish I could end it. Annie, what would you do?

—*Burning Desire*

DEAR BURNING: I think you already know what I'm going to say. But if a kick in the pants is what you're looking for, I'm happy to provide it. So here goes.

Cut it out. No more emails, no more phone calls. Exes can be friends when both parties have moved on. That is clearly not the case here. To continue this emotional affair is to risk your 40-year marriage—and for what? The "illusion of love," as you put it. That is all that Linda ever offered. Redirect your attention to bringing some passion back into your marriage. That is the real deal.

Speak Up For Sexual Health's Sake

DEAR ANNIE: This is in regards to "JP," who advised that, if someone cheats on his or her partner, everyone involved should get tested for diseases spread through sex.

One of the worst days of my nursing career was when I told a middle-aged patient that she had tested positive for a sexually transmitted disease and needed to be treated. I also told her that any partners for the last six months should be tested and treated also. She returned with:

"I have never been with anyone other than my husband! We were high school sweethearts."

I expressed my sorrow at having to tell her this but that he MUST get tested and treated also.

Her reply was: "He had a heart attack. I buried him a month ago."

I was stunned.

Please, people: If you are cheating or considering it, understand that your actions can hurt so many people.

If you've been intimate with someone other than your partner, then go to your local health department and get tested. Think of the other people in your life—people who you might never be able to make it up to.

—*Public Health Nurse*

DEAR NURSE: That is truly tragic. If "JP's" letter didn't get through to everyone, I sure hope this does. Thank you for taking the time to write.

Happiness Takes Work, Not Quick Fixes

DEAR ANNIE: My husband and I have been married for 43 years. I have a good life, or so I thought. I recently found out that he has had an affair. When I asked him about it, he told me that it was only for eight months. And he said the reason was because I would not initiate sex. Ha, that is a two-way street. Anyway, I did some checking and found out that it was for two years. He has seen her on Christmas and New Year's Eve. And he even met with her on OUR anniversary. Then I found out that he went to see her a few hours after I had major lung surgery.

He has cried and told me how sorry he is. And how dumb he was for doing this. Every day since I found this out, he has said he is sorry. But here is my problem. First, he lent her some money—not much, but $400, and she paid back $100. He has been calling her wanting the rest. I found out he called her, and he told me yes, he wants his money. I told him to forget it.

Second, he has had back surgery three times. The last one left him with numbness and weakness in both legs. And he now has some kind of erectile dysfunction. So I am wondering if he stopped seeing her to come to me so I can take care of him. We have had sex, but he is different somehow. It is not the same as it used to be, and it really makes me wonder.

How do I get over this feeling that he may still be seeing her and talking to her? I found a burner phone with her number on it. I broke it.

I don't want to go to counseling. Just some easy steps to get over all this garbage.

—Sucker-Punched in Indiana

DEAR SUCKER-PUNCHED: It's time to start punching back. Not literally, of course, but through your actions. You might not want to go to counseling, but you really don't have a choice—for your sake, not his. Your husband has treated you very unfairly, and you deserve better. Trust your gut. If you feel that things are different, then chances are things are different.

Different can be OK. While change is scary, it can also be wonderful for transformation. But you have to do the work. Figure out what makes you happy and what you want out of life. Hopefully, through therapy, you can learn to forgive your louse of a husband for what he did and move on—with him or without him. In the end, that will be your decision. But in the meantime, it is very important for you to focus on yourself.

Sadly, there is no quick fix, but if you do the emotional work each day, you will get better and better. Eventually, you will be so far removed from the feelings that he has inflicted on you that you will wonder how someone as wonderful as you ever dealt with a partner who lied and betrayed you.

Unwilling to Change His Cheating Ways

DEAR ANNIE: My husband has a long history of being unfaithful to me. He says that it isn't cheating because he can't help himself. I've forgiven him five times.

Recently, I discovered that he's been going to a website where a girl talks to him on a webcam. In exchange for their virtual time together, he buys her jewelry, clothes and other presents.

He sends her photos from his own life: for instance, pictures from when we watched fireworks with the grandkids—except the pictures are only of the fireworks, and he doesn't mention that he was with his wife and grandchildren.

I never usually pay attention to the phone bill, but this month I looked—and I found out he'd sent and received more than 17,000 text messages. He was exchanging texts with women he'd met on a dating site. He said that it isn't cheating since he's not having sex. But I think the emotional cheating is worse. I am at my wit's end. Should I just divorce him and walk away? Please help.

— *Mrs. Undesirable*

DEAR MRS.: I refuse to call you that "U" word because your husband's behavior is no reflection on you. If anything, it shows that he has issues around his own desirability. Perhaps he's so insecure he must constantly seek the validation of women he hardly knows—and/or he's suffering from sex addiction. (You can learn more about that at https://saa-recovery.org.) However, the root of his problems is irrelevant if he's not willing to seek a cure. If your husband shows no willingness to change his behavior, then leaving may indeed be the best course. Listen to your heart, and find out what it desires.

Countless Texts to Other Women

DEAR ANNIE: I am very hurt. I met my husband on a dating site, and we have been married for four years. Recently, I looked at his phone and discovered that he has texted women thousands of times.

The other day, when I saw his text message to another woman, I said that I cannot take it anymore. He said that texting is not cheating. Is that true? I am thinking about filing for divorce.

—Fed up With Texting

DEAR FED UP: You're right, and he's wrong. Whether his activities are physical or not, your husband is placing texts to these women above your feelings and cheating on you psychologically. This emotional betrayal has the same flavor as cheating because he is doing something with other women behind your back.

Before you file for divorce, talk to him. Express how much it hurts when you see all these texts with someone else and that you would like to be that close with him.

I would also suggest couples counseling. Best of luck.

Looking to Demolish this Relationship

DEAR ANNIE: My husband is in his late 50s and works in road construction. Every time that he is assigned to a job that lasts at least six to eight weeks, he always seems to start trying to pick up a female co-worker, usually in the age range of 25 to 35. He will buy them cigarettes and lunch and drinks and is super sweet to them. He texts them all day and always tells them how beautiful they looked that day. And to every single one of these women, he at some point says: "Ever since I've met you, I've really come out of my shell. Thank you."

I have tried to talk to him about it, but he just denies it every time, even as I quote to him the text messages verbatim. He doesn't know how I know that he does this. (I won't reveal my method here.) I don't know if it is something to worry about. Am I just overreacting? To me, it seems like emotional abuse.

I have to know, Annie, should I stay with him or dump his sorry butt?

—*Confused*

DEAR CONFUSED: If only he really were sorry; that's the crux of the issue. He doesn't seem to have a shred of remorse. Tell him that if he wants this marriage to work, you two need to go to marriage counseling. Otherwise, he can take his shell and get crawling.

A Yo-Yo Relationship

DEAR ANNIE: My husband and I have been married for 29 years. Three years ago, I discovered that he was having an affair. He claimed that the affair was ending anyway, that he loved me and that he wasn't interested in being with the other woman. We went to counseling, together and separately, but after about nine months, he said he wanted a divorce. I was devastated. We filled out and signed divorce papers that he had printed online, but he said he wasn't going to file them yet.

I was casually looking for an apartment to rent, not thinking he would really file the papers, but one day he walked into our bedroom and asked me whether I could give him an estimate of when I would be moving out. A few days after that, I happened to drive past a town house for sale, and within a couple of days, I had decided to buy it. Because we were not yet divorced, I had to ask my husband for help, which he gave. Amazingly, though, he asked me whether I was buying the town house for me to live in or for us!

The town house is in my name only, and I have been living here for a little over a year. Since I moved out, however, rarely has a day gone by when my husband hasn't come over to spend time with me. We spend the evenings watching TV, go out to dinner and otherwise behave like a married couple. He filed the divorce papers the day I moved out of our house, but when we both were notified of a court date, he canceled it, and the divorce was dropped. Since then, he has brought up three or four times that he wants us to get a divorce but live together like a married couple because he wants a chance to woo me back and prove how much he loves me. Each time, I was very hurt and cut off communication with him, and each time, he would plead with me to give him another chance, saying he would never bring the subject up again.

Well, guess what. Last night, he brought over divorce papers, which I signed. I told him that he'd better let the divorce proceed this time because I'm tired of this. He thinks it's no big deal to get divorced, and he doesn't understand why I'm so upset. Oh, and the kicker? He wants to retire in a year and a half and then get married again! Am I crazy, or is he?

—*Tired of the Yo-Yo*

DEAR TIRED OF THE YO-YO: You're not crazy—but it would certainly be understandable if you were a little crazy after all your husband has put you through. Though I can't say exactly what's going on in this yo-yo's head, clearly he's only thinking of himself. He's demonstrated a staggering lack of empathy.

You need to move on, but he'll make sure that's impossible as long as he's around. So it's important that you discontinue contact with him until your wounds fully heal. If you don't already have a divorce attorney, consider hiring one. He or she could be his point of contact so you don't have to be. That would free you up to focus on taking care of yourself. Start therapy again. Make your home a sanctuary. Join a gym; there's nothing like realizing your strength. Designate some "emergency contacts"—friends or family you can call when you feel as if you want to call him. Make it so that when he inevitably tries reeling you back in, he finds you've cut the string.

My Husband the Creep

DEAR ANNIE: My husband and I have been married for eight years. My first marriage ended because my ex was a serial cheater and all-around creep. "Mike" seemed to be the exact opposite. However, shortly after we were married, I found out he was checking out dating sites. I confronted him, and he deleted his accounts.

Then, about two years ago, I found out he and a 22-year-old co-worker had a sexting relationship. I was going to file for divorce, but he promised me he would stop. I insisted we go to counseling, and we went a few times. He said he had never been physically unfaithful to me. I warned him that this was strike two and that three strikes and he would be out.

A few months later, I checked his Twitter account and was disgusted by the sleazy women he was communicating with. Strike three. He pleaded with me to stay. Eventually, he deleted his Twitter account and promised to stay on the straight and narrow.

A few months ago, while paying our cellphone bill, I glanced at the record of his text messages. I found several texts sent in the middle of the night to an 18-year-old high school girl whom he used to work with. Can you tell me any good reason a 60-year-old man should be texting an 18-year-old girl he does not even work with anymore?

I am getting up the courage to confront my husband about this and to most likely go through another gut-wrenching divorce. Why am I writing to you? I guess it's just to validate my feelings—to tell me I don't deserve this. By the way, I have never cheated on him in any way. He reads your column every day in the paper. If you would agree that a 60-year-old man reaching out to girls younger than his own daughters is creepy, he might listen. But I'm not holding my breath.

—*Deja Vu in Wisconsin*

DEAR DEJA VU: If you're looking for someone to tell you that your husband's behavior is creepy, you have come to the right place. His behavior is very creepy. The first text with a 22-year-old woman from work should have tipped you off. You can't have a healthy relationship with someone who is preoccupied with relationships with others. It's time to pack your bags and head out. It might cause you pain in the short term, but in the long run, you will be liberating yourself from a lifetime of lies and deception.

Cut the Cord

DEAR ANNIE: For over four years, I was with and engaged to who I believed to be an incredible man. He was smart, funny and hardworking. We had to live in two separate states for work, but I commuted as much as I could and helped with his bills. I learned six weeks ago he has been cheating on me. I told him to go be happy.

Honestly, I meant it. Instead, he called every day, told me he wasn't with her anymore and called her every name in the book. I finally told him I couldn't take communicating every day—that he was pushing me into a nervous breakdown. Two days later, he announced their engagement. They had never broken up. He's been lying to her also.

Here's the question: We have investments together. We are stuck speaking at least once a month, but I can't believe a word he says, so I'm not sure he's actually doing what he says he's doing and protecting my interests. The other thing is I don't hate him. I don't know how to. We went through so much, and he tossed everything away with no explanation, as if our relationship and I were garbage. How do I unlove someone? How do I deal with him without getting upset?

—*Heartbroken and Betrayed*

DEAR HEARTBROKEN AND BETRAYED: First things first. Get out of your investments together so you can cut off contact with him. He sounds like a very unhappy man, and you don't need that in your life. Unloving someone takes time. Give yourself permission to grieve your loss of what you thought the future might look like. The reality is that he was not who he pretended to be, and you dodged a bullet by breaking it off with him. It will take time to see that.

Now is the time to reach out to friends and family you trust. Lean on them for support and strength. In time, your feelings will fade and you will find a man who truly deserves someone as special as you. You could also seek the help of a therapist. Best of luck to you, and remember, in the long run, it is a blessing that you are no longer with him. Your real man is waiting for you!

Annie Lane

Working Through Emotional Affair

DEAR ANNIE: I have been with my husband for 23 years now, married for the last eight. A year ago, I found out that my husband had been communicating with an old high school girlfriend without my knowledge. They ran into each other seven years ago and had been talking daily. He used his work phone so I wouldn't be able to suspect anything. She knew he was married, and that we have five kids.

He's accepted responsibility and has said he understands it is a form of cheating. He's apologized and says he has no romantic feelings for this woman. They were just friends. I called her one day to ask if she had feelings for my husband. She said she did not.

A year later, I still don't trust my husband. I feel insecure and think maybe there's something missing from our marriage that this woman provided for him. I just can't get over the betrayal. The people I have spoken with say it's not worth ending our marriage over. But I can't let it go. I've always believed cheating is a deal breaker, and that's exactly what he's done to me. I love my husband very much, but I don't think I can get past his emotional affair. Am I overreacting by considering ending my marriage for this?

—*Hurt and Confused*

DEAR HURT AND CONFUSED: It's time to examine your feelings about yourself and your marriage. It is understandable that you are hurt by what your husband did. However, he has apologized for it and stopped his relationship with her for you. Now, it is up to you to forgive. Forgiveness is a gift you give to yourself. It gives strength to move on. Though you can't change the past or go back to the same marriage you once had, you can decide what you'd like your marriage to look like from this point forward. Seek the help of a professional counselor to support you in working through this hurt and anger, and then consider marriage counseling.

Disapproving of Affair

DEAR ANNIE: I've been seeing a married man lately, and I can just tell from the looks on my friends' faces that they don't approve. The way I see it, his marital problems have nothing to do with me. He and I have a relationship that is totally separate from that, in many ways. How can I get my friends to stop judging me?

—*Miffed*

DEAR MIFFED: When you feel like a nail, everything looks like a hammer. You must be harboring at least a little guilt over this affair, or you wouldn't be seeing judgment on friends' faces.

Breaking the DNA Test News

DEAR ANNIE: Recently, my wife of nearly 50 years confessed to having had an affair that lasted more than two years with her supervisor at the time, who was twice her age.

The timing of this affair—more than 30 years ago—led me to question the paternity of our daughter. My wife was positive that I am the father, and I believed her. However, a reputable and duplicated DNA test confirmed that I am not our daughter's biological father. I am devastated, and my wife is in shock and broken.

I love her too much to do anything but continue to love her. However, in my opinion, my wife's inability at the time to think things out has led us to ask, what do we do now? Does not the biological father, now in his 80s, have a right to know he has another daughter and granddaughters? Does our daughter have the right to know her father? How do we tell her? Are there legal issues? We have a strong, healthy and now Christian family, and nobody will believe this of my wife. I feel lost in space.

—*A Broken Dad*

DEAR BROKEN DAD: Your love for your wife and ability to forgive her after all these years is beautiful. Your daughter will always be your daughter, no matter what a DNA test says. Having built your family on a strong Christian foundation doesn't mean that you or your wife never made mistakes. No matter your faith, we are all humans, and no one is perfect. Admitting your mistakes and saying you're sorry is what builds character. Start with being honest with your daughter. Consider going to a family therapist or counselor to help work through all of these new emotions. And please consult a lawyer for any legal questions. There are resources to support you and your family. Best of luck.

Your Marriage Matters Most

DEAR ANNIE: I am a single mom with two kids, who are now adults. My husband is also divorced. He and his ex-wife, "Tricia," have a 12-year-old son. The reason they divorced is that Tricia was caught cheating. But by my mother-in-law's telling, Tricia only cheated because of my husband's own wrongdoings. My mother-in-law always protects Tricia like that: shows her sympathy and insists that she is still part of the family since she's the mother of her first grandson. His other family members don't like Tricia because of what she did.

My mother-in-law and the ex are still good friends, and she always wants her to be involved in our lives.

I'm writing now because my husband's son is staying with us for a vacation. His birthday is coming up, and we're having a party for him. My mother-in-law wants Tricia to join us with the rest of her family. I feel hurt because it seems like my mother-in-law doesn't care about what I feel.

My husband also doesn't seem to care about my situation, even though I told him that I feel offended most of the time for his mother's actions. He will only look at me and say, "You should have known my mom would act this way."

—*Feeling Jealous*

DEAR FEELING JEALOUS: Inviting Tricia to her son's 13th birthday party is the gracious thing to do (assuming things are amicable enough between your husband and her). Dig deep within yourself to find the fortitude. Set your feelings aside for two hours.

Beyond the birthday party, though, it sounds as though your main problem isn't with the ex-wife but with your mother-in-law. You're afraid she's rejecting you. Rather than pouring all your thought and energy into trying to make her like you more than his ex, let it go. The relationship that matters most here is your marriage. Work on opening up communication with your husband, potentially attending a few sessions of marriage counseling together, so you can work past insecurities and develop the skills to talk to each other. When you can fully appreciate that your husband loves you and has chosen you, you won't be so concerned with what his mother thinks.

Icky Behavior

DEAR ANNIE: I just don't know what to do. My husband is always talking to and texting young girls. He's even been slapping our granddaughter on the behind and trying to make our younger granddaughter kiss him on the lips. My daughter and I both told him this behavior is unacceptable. He is no longer allowed around any of my grandchildren.

I told him that I wanted a divorce, and he said that he didn't care what I wanted. He said that he was not going anywhere.

Recently, he was also being touchy with some of the ladies where we live. Finally, I told him that I had talked to a lawyer. If he didn't straighten up, then I would sign papers and he'd be out.

So far, he has been behaving himself. But I can never trust him again. And now, on top of this, I have people telling me that he is digging in trash cans for cigarette butts. What should I do?

—*Disgraced, Disgusted*

DEAR DISGRACED: I'm so sorry you're in this awful situation. From your letter, it sounds like this has been an abrupt personality shift. That could indicate a serious health problem such as dementia, which can damage parts of the brain that impact sexual behavior. You and your husband should consult his doctor, who can diagnose any potential health issues or refer you to a specialist who can better help.

Time to Fully Commit or Quit

DEAR ANNIE: I have been with this guy off and on for 26 years. We are the best of friends. We do everything together that would have us a couple. Well, just a few weeks ago he told me he had "hooked up" with someone we both know. She is the wife of a friend who was just sent to prison. Now, she keeps texting and calling him, telling him she loves him and can't wait to feel his touch again. What really bugs me is that it sounds like the two of them were more intimate than he and I have ever been.

When I bring up how her texting him bothers me, he said that she annoys him, too, and he realizes that hooking up with her was a mistake. He doesn't acknowledge the texts that she sends and doesn't answer her phone calls. But she just doesn't get the hint.

Lately, I've started deleting some of her texts before he can read them. I texted her from my own phone to say that I'm a part of his life whether she or anyone else likes it. What more can I do to make her see that she's wasting her time thinking he's going to be with her?

—*Totally Stressed Out*

DEAR STRESSED OUT: The more useful question is why are you wasting your time on a man who won't commit. It sounds like he's not even recognized you as his girlfriend. And whether or not he replies to this other woman's text messages, he clearly gets something out of the attention, or he'd have blocked her number by now.

You deserve to be with someone who wants to be with you entirely—not halfway. In a healthy, secure and truly loving relationship, you won't feel the need to fend off other women.

Don't Quit Yet

DEAR ANNIE: Today, I wanted to share my experience with the hopes that it would enlighten you and others. Your advice to the woman was to leave her husband that has been unfaithful to her many times. My experience, however, and that of many partners of sexaholics, would say to put on the brakes. First, she should get tested for any venereal diseases, as these sexaholics are liars. Having said that, there is help for him and for her as well. If, and only if, he wants help, he should seek out a therapist who specializes in sexual addiction. I would also advise her, whether he wants help or not, to also seek a therapist who deals with partners of sexaholics. Clearly, she has a pattern of picking out partners with this behavior and she could utilize a support system for her.

It takes a long time and sometimes slips happen (on both sides) but this addiction is like any other. It can be helped with support and therapy. It may involve separation or even divorce, but it also may mean a stronger-than-ever marriage because now it is based on truth.

—*Joanie*

DEAR JOANIE: Thanks for speaking to a light at the end of this particular tunnel. I have heard from other readers who have, with treatment, been able to manage sex addictions and improve their marriages. In addition to therapy, there are support groups available, including Sex Addicts Anonymous and Sexual Recovery Anonymous.

How Can I Forgive My Cheating Partner?

Hard Truths on the Hard Drive

DEAR ANNIE: I've been with "Robby" for three years. I just moved in with him a few weeks ago, and I've been discovering some unpleasant surprises while using his computer. First, I found some racy photos saved on his hard drive. Then, I saw in his browser history that he'd been on dating sites and saw that he'd been emailing with people from dating websites, too. I asked him about it. He denies having done any of that and says he doesn't know how that stuff got on his computer and email. But the proof is right there. I don't know what to do. I don't trust him, but I love him so much. Please help me.

—*So Confused and Hurt*

DEAR SO CONFUSED: Is it possible someone has been logging onto his computer and planting incriminating photos and emails? Theoretically, sure. But it's incredibly unlikely. And it's no wonder you're confused; Robby has done nothing to help you understand. Unless and until he can tell you the truth and work to make it right by you, start packing those boxes back up.

Ditch the Two-Timer

DEAR ANNIE: I met this guy, "Bill," through work. We hit it off. He'd told me he was single. Later, I found out through a mutual colleague that Bill had a girlfriend, "Julie," a divorced lady with two kids, but he wouldn't be able to marry her because his family wouldn't approve their marriage. So, I confronted him. He stated that she was not his girlfriend and that our colleague made the whole story up. Bill and I started dating, and, after a while, I found out that he was still seeing this lady and hanging out with her. I confronted him again, and he stated that it's not going anywhere with her, and she knows that, too. I do not believe that. I think, deep inside, she thinks she is dating a loyal guy and is waiting for him to propose any minute.

I realized that Bill is just using Julie to kill time to have someone to hang out with because he doesn't want to be alone. But he doesn't want to commit to either one of us. So, when she is not available, I am available, and vice versa. I feel sorry for her because she has no clue what is happening. She is wasting her time on someone who won't commit to her. I know her name, her Facebook account, where she lives and lots more. I want to tell her the truth about Bill, but Bill will know that it was me who told her the truth. I'm scared because I don't know what his reaction will be, and he knows where I live. Should I tell her the truth about this man?

—Bad Romance

DEAR BAD ROMANCE: I commend you for wanting to help this poor woman. But it sounds as though you'd be putting yourself at risk. Focus on making a clean break from busy Bill, and trust that the other woman will see the light in time.

If you're afraid for your safety due to possible retaliation from him, call the National Domestic Violence Hotline at 1-800-799-7233 for guidance.

How Can I Forgive My Cheating Partner?

The Only Way Back from Cheating Is Through Truth

DEAR ANNIE: I met the man of my dreams about two years ago. He showed me what it felt like to be loved by a man for the first time. I was the happiest I had ever been—until about six months ago. I caught him in a hotel with another woman. She came out first and tried to make me believe he wasn't there. But the room was in his name. So, I knew he was there. I waited and, eventually, he did come outside. When he did, he had a huge grin on his face. That will forever haunt me. All he would say is that it wasn't what I thought it was.

I decided to dig a little deeper and found out he had been hiring prostitutes since the day we moved in together. He had also stayed two weeks with another woman when I went on vacation a year before. He has yet to apologize in any way. If I bring it up, then he gets mad and says that it's in the past. And wants me to believe that he's not still cheating. I love this man very much, but how do I get past this? It would be easier if he'd talk about it. He won't. He gets mad and acts like I'm the one doing wrong just by bringing it up. Any advice would help.

—*Heartbroken in Kentucky*

DEAR HEARTBROKEN: Couples can work together to heal the wounds of infidelity—but only when the partner who's been unfaithful shows remorse and a desire to change. If he not only betrayed you but won't even say sorry, then it's time to kick his sorry caboose to the curb. His behavior hasn't just been deceitful; it's been disrespectful. As painful as it might be to break up with him, you're in for a lifetime of hurt if you don't.

Annie Lane

Cut the Toxicity Out of Your Life

DEAR ANNIE: Almost four years ago, I had a double mastectomy, and five months prior to that, a complete hysterectomy! Over time, I have had 19 surgeries. Needless to say, I haven't felt very good about myself. In fact, I've felt pretty low more times than I can count.

Then I found out that my husband has been looking up ubersex, dating sites and free Facebook hookups and multiple similar sites. I don't know for sure if he has actually met with anyone. He doesn't know that I know, at least for now. I've put up with a lot throughout our relationship, including his addiction troubles.

I've never been the kind to let someone else define my worth, but I've lost any self-esteem I've ever had! I'm not a weak woman at all. I've fought hard over the last several years to be here for my family and myself.

My husband won't touch me or even look at me if I'm changing, and that hurts! This act that's so Intimate from someone so close to me has made me feel so unsexy and not wanted! My relationship has never been easy, but I've fought for it, and at times, so has he. But this time, I feel like in order to heal myself, I need to find myself by myself. His actions have really impacted me! Any insight helps.

—*Lost in My Own Head*

DEAR LOST: First things first: You are a strong woman. You survived a double mastectomy and a hysterectomy while being married to a louse. Regardless of whether he actually cheated, the fact that he is busy looking at dating sites instead of bringing you chicken soup while you recover is enough evidence to say you either need to go to counseling NOW or say goodbye.

It is completely understandable that his actions have impacted you, but now it is time to free yourself of that toxic relationship. Go to counseling with your husband and see if he can make a complete change in behavior and be there for you, or move on and find someone who sees and appreciates you for the beautiful woman you are. One of the vows we take in marriage is "in sickness and in health." He seems not to take that one seriously, for when he had addiction troubles, you stood by him, and after you had major surgeries, he left you emotionally and physically. I wish you the best of luck and have faith that you will find your self-esteem again.

Wanting to Leave After So Many Lies

DEAR ANNIE: My wife of 30 years had an affair a couple of years ago. To this day, she maintains that there was no physical contact, despite the sheer amount of text messages and phone calls; conversations usually lasting hours after I had gone to bed; my having actually caught her out with him and with her car parked at his residence on an evening she was supposed to be staying out of town with a friend.

She came home, and her explanation was that I owed him an apology because he felt threatened by me. I moved out for a while, and upon my return home, I quickly discovered a prepaid phone that only had his number. I don't believe this was a platonic relationship. I still don't trust her. I do love my wife, but I feel I'm being disrespected with her continued dishonesty. Is divorce my only option?

—*Should I Stay, or Should I Go?*

DEAR STAY OR GO: You should not threaten anyone, even if you are very upset with him or her. If the trust is gone and you want to see if you can save the marriage, the help of a professional marriage counselor is needed.

Rocky Seas Lead to Drifting Ships

DEAR ANNIE: My wife and I are drifting apart. I'm a recovering alcoholic of four years. I put her through a lot when I was drinking. When I got sober, I put my recovery first. I went to a lot of meetings of Alcoholics Anonymous and put her second. Now, she is seeing someone else.

I think at this point it's only an emotional affair, not a sexual one. But there have been times when she said she was going out with friends, and I know she went out with him. I'm not sure how I feel about it. I should be angry, and I'm not. But I don't like it—it bothers me to no end. Communication in our relationship is nonexistent. I'm not sure what to do.

—*Drifting*

DEAR DRIFTING: Let's start with congratulations on your recovery. Four years is something to be very proud of. It sounds like your wife still harbors resentment and pain from your drinking days. I might suggest that she attend Al-Anon meetings to help her better understand why you have to put your recovery first. My guess is that you know that if you didn't, everything else in your life would fall apart, including your marriage.

The past is past, and it sounds like you have made amends. Communication is key in any marriage. It's been so long that you and your wife might need to rebuild these communication channels to make this work. Take action and seek the help of a professional marriage counselor. If your wife refuses to go, then you should go yourself. Sometimes, when people use alcohol to numb their feelings for years, they lose touch with them. It's time to go to a therapist or counselor and rediscover how you do feel about things.

And keep going to meetings. As they say in AA, the program works if you work it.

Hidden Grief

DEAR ANNIE: I'm a married woman who has been in a secret relationship for three years with a co-worker of mine. My boyfriend died by suicide last week, and my world has been turned upside-down. I was the last person he texted, and he wanted me to come over. I told him I couldn't. A couple of hours later, he was gone. I have been crying uncontrollably ever since, and no one understands why.

He, too, was in a relationship, and I was led to believe she knew about us and was OK with our relationship. My husband does not know. Because I'm the "other woman," I had no say in anything after his passing and wasn't able to keep anything of his as a memory. My question is this: Would it be wrong to reach out to his family? They do not know about our relationship, and I wonder if I should tell them. I also want a few belongings (just a T-shirt, if anything!), but would it be wrong to ask?

—*Grieving "Girlfriend"*

DEAR GRIEVING GIRLFRIEND: There is a lot to unpack in your letter. First, I am sorry that you lost your boyfriend to suicide. It is truly a tragedy when someone takes their own life. As far as wanting to tell his family that he was having an affair with you, I might hold off for a while. They are grieving the loss of their son.

This might be a good time to get into therapy yourself. First, to understand why you felt the need to stay in your marriage, and then to process the trauma of losing your boyfriend to suicide. Assuming you still want to stay married, you owe it to your husband to get into marriage counseling and to come clean with him and hope that you can rebuild your relationship based on trust and forgiveness.

Wanting to Be Happy

DEAR ANNIE: I have been married for over 20 years to a woman who has been a good mom, but not a woman I am in love with. I care about her tremendously, but I have lost all interest in her romantically. She refuses to work to help with the rising cost of living and impending college tuition for two older teenage kids. She doesn't really keep a clean house. I do as much or more of the cooking—probably as I prefer to. She wears T-shirts and, half the time, no makeup when I get home.

She just doesn't seem to care about pleasing her husband. I've asked about counseling for years, but she blames me for not going. "You wouldn't do it," she says.

I want to live the rest of my life happy and in love. The thought of living without being in love for the rest of my life is terrifying. I'm a romantic and need that spark.

Then along comes another woman. Yeah, same old story, I know. There is absolutely nothing going on between us, but I admit I wish there were.

So, I can see what's out there that I want to be with. But I'm married and feel obligated to that person who helped build a family. To say I am conflicted is an understatement.

I know if I left, then there is zero guarantee and little chance of the other woman being interested. Yet, to be able to try to find happiness, to give that a chance, that is starting to seem worth it. My marriage has been going through this for 15 of the 20-plus years. It's not new. So being in a highly emotional state, I keep thinking I need to choose between finding passion or remaining in stale obligation. I need advice. I don't want to hurt my wife. I don't want to hurt my kids, although I think they are old enough to deal with me leaving. I want to be happy.

—Conflicted

DEAR CONFLICTED: Marriage is a two-way street, and I'm sure your wife is not thrilled about being married to someone who is highly critical of her. She can probably sense that you don't find her attractive romantically and is sad about that. It could be part of the reason that she seems to have given up looking nice for you or cooking you a nice meal.

Marriage is a give and take, and it sounds like neither of you is giving, and you're both unhappy. At this point, marriage counseling would be the first step to take.

When your wife says about marriage counseling, "You wouldn't do it," is she right? If so, look in the mirror. You were close during the first five years of your marriage. With professional help, the two of you might rekindle your early romance. It will take a lot of work, but I can't think of anything more important. If during your counseling you decide that you don't want to make it work, then set her free. No one should have to be in a relationship where the person outwardly says they are not "in love" with their spouse. But remember that there is a difference between love and lust.

Affairs of the Heart

DEAR ANNIE: My husband had an emotional affair with his boss. He texted her, called her and tried to go out with her. She did not reciprocate and, as far as I know, kept it strictly business. He told her his feelings, but she told him she was not interested. He quit his job after that but continued to text her, asking her to go out. She didn't reply.

When I found out, he told me he just wanted to have sex with her, and her not giving in made him pursue her more. Now, I feel in second place in my marriage. Would he still be here if had she had said yes? What were his true feelings?

They only worked together and were never physically intimate. I am lost and don't know what to do.

—*Lost and Alone*

DEAR LOST: What your husband did to you was disgraceful. You have every right to be upset and hurt. His intentions were enough for you to leave. You should seek the help of a professional marriage counselor to decide whether it is worth staying together. Best of luck.

Broken After Baby

DEAR ANNIE: I'm a 24-year-old new mom to a gorgeous son. But I discovered that my husband was—and I'm 100% sure still is—cheating on me with someone who I thought I could trust. She has known us since I found out I was pregnant.

On the day that I brought my son home from the hospital, she was the first person to hold him outside of my husband and me. He keeps saying that she's distancing herself from him because he turned her down for sex, but I went through his phone and saw a message from her saying to come over, and he said he was on his way.

I don't know what to do. I love him so much, and he's the father of my son. Help please.

—Shocked and Saddened

DEAR SHOCKED AND SADDENED: Congratulations on the birth of your gorgeous son. I am so sorry that your husband is unable to be present for you and your newborn. Sadly, some men feel jealous of a newborn and sometimes act out. This awareness in no way excuses his behavior.

While you can't control his actions, you can control yours. Stop snooping on his phone and start having real and honest conversations with him about his infidelity. If this is to work, you have to seek the help of a counselor.

Annie Lane

Suffering in Silence

DEAR ANNIE: My husband was very abusive and made me feel worthless. I started an affair with a married man. Even after my husband died, the affair continued, as I was all alone without support from my family and the abusive relationship had taken away most of my friends.

Fast-forward 20 years. The man I had the affair with had a procedure that failed, and he was given only a few weeks to live.

During those few weeks, he contacted friends and family and sent messages to everyone except me. It's like I was punched in the gut. I know I was the other woman and couldn't be with him in his final days, but a short call or even a social media emoji to say goodbye would have meant the world to me. After all those years, I don't know if I meant anything to him. Words were never spoken. I grieve in silence.

I tried counseling a few times, but they take five sessions before they even get to the heart of the problem, and with co-pays, I just can't afford it. The point I want to make is to tell a person how you feel no matter what the circumstances.

—*Silent Grief*

DEAR SILENT GRIEF: Stick with the counseling. If you can't afford the co-pays, see if your therapist can work something out for you. In addition, find a group to help you process your grief. There are many out there. Rest assured that his being with you for all that time shows he cared about you. In fact, showing someone is a lot more meaningful than telling them. Words are just words; his actions spoke louder than his silence.

I am hopeful that you will find a new love. As you work through your grief, try and find someone who is not taken so there is love and honesty in your relationship from the beginning.

Marriage Is More Than Being There

DEAR ANNIE: I have been married to a caring, sweet, very cool woman for the last 13 years. We have four children. Like all marriages, we've had our ups and downs, but I thought we were solid.

A few months ago, she started spending time with an old friend, "Jimmy," who is a shady guy. One night after spending time with Jimmy, she came home, sat beside me on the couch, and calmly told me that she wanted to separate and that she had already set her Facebook status to single. She claimed that I was manipulating her. While I've seen how manipulative her family can be, I've never been manipulative toward her, at least not intentionally. I've always supported her emotionally, and I've never withheld money or anything like that.

But when I told her that I didn't think I was being manipulative, she said she really had just fallen out of love. She talked about how I wasn't affectionate with her; I didn't hold her hand. Well, I have been sleeping on the couch a lot of nights the last few years, only due to my not wanting to roll on our 3-year-old, who slept in our bed almost every night.

We have not been intimate the last few years except when she was tipsy and wanted to. I was not into it but went along with it. But if it was more affection and handholding that she'd wanted, I wish she had just told me. I guess I overlooked the little things.

I think about our four children and what our splitting up would mean for them. I worry about my wife's stability and, consequently, our youngest daughter's safety. I refuse to initiate the divorce on my end because we took a vow. Or should I just give up? Do you think I could find someone who would like me for me and accept the kids? I am probably one of the easiest people to get along with, and I always try to do the right thing.

—*Heavyhearted Husband*

DEAR HEAVYHEARTED: I commend you for taking your wedding vows to heart. But being a good partner isn't just about staying in it; it's about staying present for it. Of course, your intimacy has suffered when you've been spending nearly every night on the couch. But if this is really the first time that your wife is raising any of these issues with you, then you both owe it to your marriage to try to work through them. Ask her to attend couples counseling with you. And if she insists on divorce, don't rush into your next relationship. Work on developing your self-esteem and communication skills first, so you'll be bringing your best, healthiest self to the table.

Fidelity to Facebook Over Matrimony

DEAR ANNIE: We are on our second marriage and in our 60s. I believe he loves me, but Facebook is coming between us.

I do not think he would go out and cheat on me, but he loves friends/women on his computer. I have not found anything real bad yet on Facebook, but he spends nearly all day and night on it. That's his life.

He used to ask pretty, single younger women to be friends. I had a fit and told him it had better stop, and it has. But that hasn't stopped his obsession with staying on Facebook.

Am I overreacting for getting upset when he finds an attractive woman and "likes" nearly everything on her page, including when she's posting photos of herself?

I have seen him chatting with women, but he's not saying anything sexual.

However, there have been regular conversations with only a few that he has known, and they were single.

I tell him that it could open doors, and women are more emotional and can read into the conversation as flirting. He assures me that's not the case. But all his time is spent on his phone, and we are still newlyweds!

I have been having serious thoughts about leaving him. I have made him realize how this makes me feel. One other thought is this: Maybe he is erasing evidence?

He used to consistently talk about it until I put a stop to it. He is aware of how I feel. I have even let him know I'm thinking about leaving, which he says he doesn't want. He says I am just a jealous person.

—*Marriage Falling*

DEAR MARRIAGE FAILING: It's not just Facebook that is coming between the two of you. It is his lack of respect for you. He should not be chatting with other women on Facebook and distracted. You can't have a relationship with someone when you're only seeing the top of his head because he never has his eyes off the computer or phone.

Part of intimacy is connecting face to face with eye contact, and if his eyes are glued to a screen with other women on them, you have every right to be upset. He could be addicted to the screen, but, like all addictions, he has to want to take steps necessary to reform—both for his mental health and for your marriage. And to gain the strength to break this addiction, he'll need to be able to share honestly with a wife who is willing to listen. I strongly advise that you seek marriage counseling soon if you want to stay in this marriage.

13 Years of Bad Luck

DEAR ANNIE: I'm confused about an issue that involves my husband. We have been separated for 13 years. We try to work things out all the time, but now, suddenly, he said I cheated on him. He also said that all I do is lie to him. He said he doesn't want to listen to me when I tell him the truth. He listens to everybody else.

So, should I keep trying, or should I just get the divorce and move on with my life and find someone new? Please help me.

—*Confused*

DEAR CONFUSED: The answer is pretty clear. After 13 years of what sounds like a toxic relationship, it is time to either commit to marriage counseling or to get divorced. Staying in limbo, continuing to accuse each other of cheating and fighting all the time is not healthy for anyone. Best of luck to you.

Fiancee's Fishy Friendship

DEAR ANNIE: I am about to get married to a woman I am still madly in love with, five years after we first met. Within two months after our first date, we told each other we were in love with each other and wanted to date each other exclusively. Yet, within four months, she was lying to me, going off for a night here and a night there, claiming to visit her sister, but actually staying with a married man she's known since high school—a man with whom, she has admitted to me, she cheated on her late husband.

During our first year of dating, she tried reassuring me that it's "emotional, not physical." Is that supposed to be better?! I told her she knows how I feel, and I'd appreciate her not talking to this man, at this point.

Yet, one day she was showing me something on her phone and accidentally showed me photos of them together. I looked at her phone later and saw the photos were dated recently. She lied to me about her whereabouts on those days. I have confronted her about her ongoing relationship with this man. She refuses to admit they still see each other.

We have lots of years and dating histories under both our belts. I realize that. I am not trying to control her, but I am also not willing to share her—not in this way. Is it wrong to ask to see her phone records to see if she is still talking and texting with him before I say "I do"? Is just having the question in my head enough that I should call it off?

—*Looking for Information*

DEAR LOOKING FOR INFORMATION: Reviewing her call logs might provide you with temporary relief, but it wouldn't actually heal the fractured trust. In fact, in the long term it could just make things worse, by reinforcing a dynamic where you feel compelled to play private investigator to quell any suspicions.

Unfortunately, it does sound as though your suspicions are well-founded. It's OK for our significant others to have friends of the opposite sex or even to be platonic friends with exes. But there is a difference between a friendship and an emotional affair. It sounds like your fiancee is swept up in the latter and has been for some time. Given her history with this man, it's reasonable that you would feel uncomfortable with her spending time with him. It's hurtful that she continues to do so after you've expressed your discomfort. And the fact that she lies about seeing him—that is indeed major cause for pause. Unless you can say "I do" with all your heart, then it's better not to say it.

Honesty Needed in a Healthy Marriage

DEAR ANNIE: My husband doesn't spend time with me anymore. We have been together for eight years and married for three. We were inseparable most of that time, but, all of a sudden, he doesn't want me around. He says most married people hardly ever hang out. He tells me the honeymoon is over.

I have tried everything. At marriage counseling, he puts on a show and tries to make me look bad. He mostly ignores my calls and texts when he leaves, and when he does respond, it's very nasty.

I'm not sure if he is cheating or not. I don't think I want to be married to him anymore. How do I handle this? Is asking for a divorce reasonable? How do you do that?

—*Still Unsure*

DEAR UNSURE: Are you telling the marriage counselor that you feel he puts on a show and tries to make you look bad? It is important to be completely honest during your counseling sessions or else they won't work. Once you have said all of that during your therapy sessions, and you still want a divorce, then you can most certainly ask for one. Honesty, love and communication are all pillars for a healthy marriage, and you deserve a man who understands that.

You Can, and Should, Escape

DEAR ANNIE: My husband and I have been married for 24 years, and we have two adult kids who no longer live in our household.

My husband has always treated me as if I were his maid. I am told to do all the housework. I don't mind, but sometimes a little help is nice. When he's not upset, he's the sweetest man.

About three years ago, he made me quit my job because I cheated on him. He made me delete all social media, and I was unable to take individual pictures of myself.

We have been having lots of disagreements, and one day in our home, he hit me. That left me with bruises and a bad headache because he hit me on the head. I told him I didn't love him and wanted to divorce him. As soon as I said that, he promised he would never hit me again and that he would be a better person in the future.

He always does this. He slaps me and then promises he will never do it again. And then he does it again, and I fall into his little game—again. After the most recent incident, he bought me a belt and clothing that I have been wanting so that I would forgive him.

What do I do to get away from him? I have no money or job. How do I leave this man?

—*Trapped By a Monster*

DEAR TRAPPED: It might feel like you are trapped because 24 years of living with a man who is abusive is a long time. But you are not trapped. There is help available. There are many local and national hotlines available to help women in your exact situation. I encourage you to contact the National Domestic Violence Hotline at 1-800-799-7233 or chat with someone via their website (https://www.thehotline.org). The National Coalition Against Domestic Violence is another great resource at https://ncadv.org/get-help. If you feel like you are in immediate danger, call 911. Just remember that you have the power to leave the cage that you feel trapped in. There are groups and people out there.

Not Worth the Trouble

DEAR ANNIE: I have been seeing this guy, "Roy," for a year and a half. When we are together, all he wants to do is hook up. He comes to my house all the time, but he never invites me to his. I actually still have no idea where he lives: I know the vicinity, but no specifics. He says he wants to keep some parts of his life private. And he only calls and talks to me on the phone when he is heading to or from work, but never when he's at home. He tells me he loves me, but I'm not buying it. What do you think?

—*Help Me*

DEAR HELP ME: I think that there's a 99% chance he's married and a 100% chance he's not worth your time. End it ASAP. Breaking things off is rarely easy, but I guarantee that you will not regret this in the long term.

Couple Is Worlds Apart Before Tying the Knot

DEAR ANNIE: My fiancee and I have been together for six years, and I am having a hard time understanding where I fit in her life. She claims to love me, but lately, her actions just don't say that. She puts everyone ahead of me. Last Christmas, we went to her mom's on the other side of the country and her mom told her she had to introduce me as her friend.

She still has contact with her ex-husband, who, after we got together, asked her to send him inappropriate pictures of herself. She contacts him when she gets drunk, about every six months. Then she lies about it, even when I catch her talking to him.

Her daughter who is 30 just had her fourth child, and my fiancee devotes time and money to her. Her daughter makes more money than both of us. We spent over $250 on a baby shower for her daughter and only about $50 on my son and his wife when they were expecting their first child.

I just feel like I am being used and taken advantage of. We bought a car together last summer, and she put it solely in her name. Every time I ask if we can get my name on the title, she says, "Sure, you pay for it." I think we should go halves like we did paying for the car.

—*Scared and Confused*

DEAR SCARED AND CONFUSED: Actions speak louder than words, and it sounds like she is being selfish and entitled. But it is up to you to stick up for yourself and say that you are not going to give half the money if she doesn't put the car in your name. As far as how much money was spent on her daughter versus your son, try not to count pennies. It's about the celebration of the baby and the love that is present, not the amount of money spent on the celebration.

I suggest you both go to counseling before you tie the knot. Best of luck to you.

Lack of Faith in Long-Distance Relationship

DEAR ANNIE: About six months ago, my boyfriend, "Jordan," relocated to another state for work. We've talked about my eventually moving there, too, so we could be together, but we've held off making firm plans. He says he needs more time to settle in to life there. He also says he wants to be positive he sees himself at this job long term before I uproot my life, too.

He visited twice within the first month after moving, but in the past five months, he's visited only once. I went out there once a couple of months ago. We do talk on the phone or video chat every other day, which helps.

The reason I'm writing is this. A friend of mine was recently in Jordan's town for work. She is single and uses a dating app that shows people within a few-mile radius. While she was on her trip, she was scrolling through profiles, when she came across Jordan and recognized him. (She's never met him in real life, but she'd seen photos of us.) She sent me a screenshot. I was shocked. I asked her to connect with him on the app to see what he said. He messaged her back almost immediately—but not because he recognized her as a friend of mine. He thought she was just a random woman, and he started chatting her up and asking what she was up to.

Devastated, I called him immediately and asked for an explanation. He said that he was just using the app to make friends and that if it made me uncomfortable, he would delete his account. I told him I thought that was a good idea. I'm wondering whether I'd be a fool to trust this man again.

—Fooled Once

DEAR FOOLED ONCE: You know the saying, so I won't remind you of the rest. Don't give Jordan another chance to break your trust. That dating app is not meant for making friends, and this man is not meant for you. As soon as you accept that, you'll be one step closer to finding someone who is.

The Other Women

DEAR ANNIE: I am an attractive and well-educated divorced woman. Recently, a man whom I dated several years ago contacted me. We are both 70. Our reunion was great. We have been getting along very well and communicating daily ever since. We live across the country from each other. He invited me to his home, where I was his guest for three weeks. When we were alone, we had a wonderful time. We have great chemistry and enjoy each other's company, sense of humor and personality. He tells me that he loves me. I love him, too.

My problem is that during my visit, it became apparent that he has numerous female "friends" (most single, some married) who are neighbors. He talked to them many times a day. They called constantly, and he took the calls privately. He even stopped in the middle of our being intimate to take calls from these women. He confides everything to them and refuses to say "no" to them.

On my last night with him, we had a romantic evening for just the two of us planned at home. He told his "harem" (as he calls his female friends) about our plans, and the women immediately told him they were coming over because they wanted to say goodbye to me. Instantly, his mob of postmenopausal women showed up. A married woman whose husband was out of town kissed my boyfriend on the lips several times, and he kissed her back, in front of me. This was very disrespectful, and it makes me wonder what they do when they are alone with each other, which they sometimes are. None of the women said "goodbye" to me, which was their excuse for monopolizing our evening. Actually, I'm pretty sure it was just a power play on the women's part, to keep my boyfriend and me from having a romantic last evening together.

After they left, I calmly complained to my boyfriend about how he and the married woman had kissed. He said that it was a "Southern thing" and that he was tired of our "discussions." He said the married woman is a "wonderful Southern girl" and said I'd better get along with her because I'll be seeing a lot of her. He berated me because I wanted to spend my last night alone with him and not drinking with the neighbor women.

I love my boyfriend and don't want to lose him, but his female friends are his first priority, and it makes me feel as though my feelings and opinions mean nothing to him. This is the only thing we disagree on. How should I handle this situation?

—Cock of the Walk's Chick

DEAR COCK OF THE WALK'S CHICK: I don't see this proud peacock putting down his plumes any time soon. He seems to love strutting his stuff, lavished with female attention 24/7. More troubling than the flirtatious behavior is the way he reacted when you expressed your concern and frustration. Such dismissiveness shows a fundamental lack of respect for your feelings. If he's not willing to hear you out and do what he can to make you more comfortable with his heavily female flock, then it's time for you to fly the coop.

Eroded Trust

DEAR ANNIE: My fiance and I want to go back to the way we were, but it is more of a struggle for me than for him. We are planning to get an apartment together, but it is hard for me to be around him without getting upset. I have been going through a lot lately, and finding out that my fiance was lying to me was one of the worst things that has happened. At first, it was something minor, and I just chose to keep my mouth shut, but the next morning he was on his phone, and I saw pictures of naked women that he tried to hide fast. I tried to get the truth out of him, but he lied.

We went to the lake to talk about it, and it just kept escalating. He's been doing it for seven months. I found out and was actually contacting someone to get these pictures. This is cheating, isn't it? He also had multiple accounts for stuff like that which he had to pay for. He promised not to do it again, but I struggle to believe it when he continues to lie to me about different things. I want to move on and be happy with him, but when something similar comes up, I break down. What should I do?

—Confused and Lost

DEAR CONFUSED AND LOST: Of course, you break down when something similar happens. It is unacceptable for your fiance to lie to you and have other women send him naked pictures. Fool me once, shame on you; fool me twice, shame on me. The best way to move on and be happy with him is to go to counseling together. You can't build a successful marriage if there is a lack of trust. Stay firm with your boundaries in the relationship. Until that's settled, don't marry the bum. Best of luck to you both.

Seeing a Married Man

DEAR ANNIE: I have been seeing the same man for 18 years. I say "seeing" because he is married. "Patrick" and I have been messing around together for a long time. Many times throughout the years, I've told him that he should really think about what he was doing since he was a married man. His response alternates between, "She and I are pretty much done"—clearly a lie—and "I don't know how I can love two women at once, but I want to." I tell him that he can't. We've known each other for so long now that he is one of my best friends. I want to end our romantic relationship, but I'd like to keep him as a friend. He says he won't have it that way. He continues to call and come over. How do I make him see that we can have a friendship and nothing more?

—No More Messing Around

DEAR NMMA: Even if you two did somehow manage to cease being intimate—a big if—a continued relationship is not a good idea. You'd just be going from a physical affair to an emotional one.

Show yourself the love and respect that this man has never been able to muster for you, and stop seeing him. There is someone out there for whom you will be more than enough.

Slept with Wife's Nieces

DEAR ANNIE: I live in a small town with my wife of 33 years. My wife has a large family, most of whom live in the same state as us. Two of her siblings had daughters the same age who grew up like sisters. Last summer her two nieces came to stay with us for a week while on a break from college. It turned out her nieces were hard-partying, dope-smoking, heavy-drinking types.

One day, while my wife was at work and I was working from home, they got me to party with them. We got pretty wasted and ended up all hooking up. The same thing happened the very next day. I know they liked seducing their aunt's husband, and I had a mind-blowing experience.

I assumed they were old enough to be discreet, but they weren't. A few weeks later one of them told another family member, and the news made it back to my wife. My wife was beyond upset. She told me to move out, but I refused. Since then, she has made my life a living hell.

I never wanted to destroy our marriage, but the allure of two young women is a fantasy most men cannot refuse. I never believed two sexual exploits could destroy my marriage of 33 years. I am not seeing a way to fix this. Any suggestions?

—*Regretful*

DEAR REGRETFUL: There are so many layers of wrongness here that I don't even know where to begin. You cheated on your wife. You cheated on her again. And the cherry on this creeptastic cake: You cheated on her with your nieces. (Yes, they are *your* nieces, too, even if not by blood.) What you did was profoundly hurtful, no matter which way you slice it.

I usually tell partners working past infidelity to try couples counseling. But for that to work, the cheater actually has to feel remorse—and despite your letter's signature, it seems like the only thing you regret is getting caught. If you can't appreciate how deeply you've hurt your wife, my only advice is to honor her wishes and pack your bags.

A New Beginning Up North

DEAR ANNIE: Please help me. I am in my mid-40s and have been with a man for seven and a half years. He has four children who I absolutely adore. His youngest is 12. We started dating when she turned 5. We have had them full time for the past seven years. I have gotten pregnant five times with this man. There were three miscarriages and two other babies who passed away due to complications at birth. My son had no lungs; he was born at 20 weeks. My daughter passed away in 2017 at eight days old.

This man has never had a single conversation with me about any of the babies that passed away. But he will talk to family members and co-workers freely about it.

He cheated on me at least two times that I know of, though he denies it to this day.

This past October, I moved six hours away from our home in

Massachusetts up to the Canadian border. He and the kids were supposed to come, but he pulled out at the last minute and has left me in limbo with where we stand.

I cry a lot over missing the older kids back home.

Please help me to understand why I'm holding onto something that is a lost cause.

In addition to being untrustworthy, untruthful and uncommunicative, he is not very kind, appreciative or affectionate toward me. He would often diminish my feelings and make me second-guess my own feelings. He has never stuck up for me or backed me up, ever.

When I try to communicate with him, I'll say something like, "Hey, can we talk?" and he says, "We are talking."

Not only did I take care of him and his kids for the past seven years. I also drove him to work and picked him up everyday with not so much as a thank you.

My main question is, what in the world is wrong with me? Why am I more concerned with what he wants than what I want? Why am I holding on to a loveless, unhappy relationship?

I love living up North. It's beautiful. I have no intention of ever going back to Massachusetts. I truly feel like I lived in a foreign land my whole life and I'm finally home.

Please give it to me straight. I have been through a lot. I can handle it.

—*Feeling Sad in Northern Maine*

DEAR FEELING SAD: You have already had to handle a great deal of neglect and abuse in your relationship, and now it is time to exit stage left as soon as possible. I'm almost positive you know the answer to your question, but you have to say to yourself, "Enough is enough." You are holding onto this loveless and unhappy marriage because it has become a habit.

It is difficult to change even if we know that changing is the best thing for ourselves. The very fact you wrote me this letter signals that you are ready for a new beginning. Leaving him will take courage and might be very uncomfortable, but like most worthwhile endeavors, if you put in the commitment and hard work, the payoff will be immense. You will no longer have to suffer.

Seeking the help of a trained professional therapist will help you move forward powerfully, learn more about setting boundaries and discover how worthy you are of love and respect.

Husband Wants to Reconcile After Affair

DEAR ANNIE: My husband and I have been having a rough time. He cheated on me with a young woman and got her pregnant. I think this was her goal, secretly. She knew he had a wife and wanted him to leave me.

Anyway, the baby will be 1 soon, and now that my husband is seeking reconciliation, I feel stuck in the middle. I've already been through my hurt stage and would hate to go through it again. What should I do?

—*Betrayed*

DEAR BETRAYED: What you want to do. Whether you decide to stay or go, you'll have made a valid choice.

I will say, infidelity does not have to be the end. Many couples have worked past betrayals and come out the other side stronger than ever, with the help of couples' counseling. If you and your husband enroll in marriage counseling, this could be the case for you. But if you are past that point, mentally, I wouldn't blame you for leaving. Trite but true, listen to your heart.

Husband Talking to My Best Friend

DEAR ANNIE: I own a bar with my best friend. We work great together. I've been married for five years, and yesterday, my business partner showed me messages from my husband. He gave her his phone number and said if she ever wants to talk, she should call. He is in no way associated with our bar. They are friends through me. I am very upset he did this. I confronted him, and he said he was just being nice. However, I'm still mad and hurt he did this. Should I just overlook this as his being friendly, or do I have a reason to be upset?

—*Aggravated*

DEAR AGGRAVATED: These sorts of situations can function as Rorschach tests for relationships: What you see can reveal a lot about your headspace. There's nothing inherently wrong with your husband reaching out to your business partner, so it's worth asking yourself why your first instinct was to suspect something inappropriate. Are there past trust issues that you haven't resolved? (Remember that "trust" doesn't just mean trusting each other not to cheat but also trusting that you can be vulnerable.)

Or perhaps your husband knew that your friend would show you the messages, and he was trying to get your goat. Or maybe he was flirting with her, as you suspected.

Whatever the case, the only way you'll find the real answer—and a real solution—is through open and honest conversation with your husband. Marriage counseling can create the space for that to happen, and it can also help you identify the path forward. Give it a try.

Reeling from Wife's Affairs

DEAR ANNIE: I found out a month ago that my wife has been sleeping with a plethora of men that she's met on a dating app. Her profile says she's single and that she also has a college degree, neither of which is true. She told me she is in love with another man. After I spoke to the man's wife, who did not know, she explained that her husband had cheated on her before and was living in their basement. She also said they have five children together and just declared bankruptcy. My wife was serious when she told me she was madly in love with him, missed him and wanted a future with this man. A future?

I uncovered her indiscretions about a month ago when I found all of the evidence on her cellphone. That night, I asked her to leave, and she did. I thought she was going to her parent's house, but I'm not sure where she went that night. I think she had a lot of options.

We have two sons, ages 12 and 14. I informed them that their mother had been cheating on me and that we are getting a divorce. In front of the kids, she pulled a butcher knife on me and threatened me because she wanted her phone. My 14-year-old son had to disarm her.

I was completely blindsided by everything that has happened. The boys live with me because of continuity in their lives and school. I have gotten them therapy as well as confided with their principal to see the school psychologist. My grieving emotions swing between anger and depression. I am praying I finally reach acceptance.

She pretends everything is OK in front of the boys. She took them out to dinner last week and asked if I wanted to join them. I declined because I didn't want to confuse the boys more. After being with her for 20 years and 12 years of marriage, the last thing I said to her before she left was, "I have no idea who you are."

I have been doing good by my sons, but I can see the depression on their faces. I don't know anyone who has experienced something this crazy, and I, too, am getting therapy.

How do I get past all of this? How do I stay strong to get through my divorce, and most importantly, how do I make sure my sons will be OK?

Does she have a multiple personality disorder? My therapist told me to stop trying to understand craziness. She said that we don't even understand crazy—we only recognize it.

Help! What do I need to do to bring normalcy back to me and my sons and get to that acceptance stage where whatever and whoever she is becomes indifferent and irrelevant to me?

—Crushed Spirit

DEAR CRUSHED SPIRIT: You certainly have been through trauma, and it takes time to heal from traumas. You're taking some important steps in getting support for you and your sons. Your therapist is correct in pointing out that you can't fully understand why your wife did what she did, but you can understand yourself and how you respond to the situation. Be kind and patient with yourself and your sons. Don't expect to get to the acceptance stage right away; just know that it will take time.

You are grieving the loss of your marriage. While there might not be people who have your exact situation, there are divorce support groups for fathers. I would suggest you look up a local support group.

I am so sorry that you are going through this, but you sound like an amazing father and a good person. It won't be right away, but if each day you work on your grief and trauma, then, before you know it, you and your sons will be feeling good again and experiencing joy. The is one of those situations where it is worth reminding yourself, each day, that life is a cinch by the inch and hard by the yard.

Ditching the Cheating Boyfriend

DEAR ANNIE: My boyfriend and I have been together for 10 years. Everything was good until three years ago when a woman contacted me to tell me that she'd been seeing him. She apologized to me for it. After we got off the phone, I found her on Facebook and realized that they'd been "liking" each other's posts for years. She even posted a photo of them together, and someone had commented making a sexual joke about them. They'd both replied and laughed.

So, I confronted my boyfriend, and he stopped—or so I thought. Then, six months ago, I found charges on his credit card statement for some local hotel! I confronted him, and he brushed it off, said it hadn't been him.

We have smart security cameras at our front and back door, and ever since I confronted him about the middle-of-the-night hotel charges, he's disabled my ability to access the camera feeds from my phone. But I can always tell when he's with her because he won't answer his phone. (Otherwise, he always answers his phone.)

I just hate the thought that the last 10 years were for nothing.

—Had It Up to Here

DEAR HIUTH: Make decisions based on your future, not on your past. You're caught up in the sunk cost fallacy—continuing your current relationship just because you've already spent so much time in it and don't want it to have been a waste. The thing is, it wasn't really a waste. Consider the good moments you've had, even with your boyfriend. Consider the tough, character-building moments, too. It's all added up to a meaningful period of growth and lessons you can take into the next decade—after leaving this lecher in the last. Which you must do, pronto.

Abuse and Another Man

DEAR ANNIE: I'm a mom and have been married for nearly six years. But for the past few years, my husband and I have not been on the same path. We can't communicate without fighting, bickering, arguing, etc. Our sex life has been nonexistent. And I have tried talking and suggesting that we do more things together. I have even tried losing weight because I thought maybe the problem was that I was no longer attractive. I tried everything that I could think of. And some days, I just lay in a different room, balled up and crying.

About a year ago, I started a new job and met a man with whom I clicked almost instantly. Eventually, this co-worker gave me his number and asked if I wanted to go fishing sometime. That night, I told my husband that another man had offered me his phone number and wanted to take me fishing. I hoped he would see that he needed to step up to the plate before something happened. Instead, he flipped out and started accusing me of trying to control him. He started throwing things around the house—something he does a lot when things don't go his way, often leaving me with bruises and/or him with bruises due to my trying to defend myself. His tantrum that night was the final straw. I decided to take my new colleague up on the fishing trip.

We became close friends but never did anything physical. Then, one day, I found out my husband had been exchanging racy messages with women online. That's when I decided to go ahead and give my body to this new friend. It was nice. It made me feel like a woman again, not like a jacket that's sitting in the closet waiting to be worn.

We continued seeing each other and sleeping together for a few months. But last month, after a night out with him, I confessed everything to my husband. He was upset, of course, but in due time he came around and said he wanted to work things out. Well, that was three months ago, and my husband and I still haven't been intimate. I see no signs of things changing between us. In fact, they've gotten more distant, and I've noticed he now uses a lock code on his phone and computer.

My lover, meanwhile, is waiting in the wings for me to make my decision.

—Between a Rock and Hard Place

DEAR BETWEEN: More than anything, I'm concerned about your husband's physical aggression. No matter your differences, it is unacceptable for him to hurt you or even knowingly endanger you as he does when he hurls things around the house in a rage. But rather than further engage him right now, I encourage you to reach out to the National Domestic Violence Hotline at 1-800-799-7233 for guidance in planning your next steps.

How Can I Forgive My Cheating Partner?

Finding Love in All the Wrong Places

DEAR ANNIE: I have let myself get involved with a significantly younger guy. To make matters worse, I'm married. In my defense, before I even started talking to this other guy, my husband and I had come to a place in our marriage where we were more like roommates than husband and wife. We didn't even share the same bedroom (which was his decision). He never showed me affection of any kind. We spoke to each other, but that was it.

I started socializing with men on social media, and I must admit I did get taken by a scammer for $12,000, which I shouldn't have never let happen. But I have met this great guy on another site. He lives in Nigeria and is younger than me. I know Nigeria has a bad track record for scammers, but this guy really doesn't seem like he would be into that stuff.

As for my husband ... I care for him and don't want to keep hurting him but my love for him isn't the way it should be. Yet, I can't bring myself to leave him.

The guy in Nigeria begs me to fly to see him. We FaceTime each other and talk on the phone so much and text each other when he's not working. We are constantly on the phone—or we were, anyway. Lately, I have noticed that often I text him, call him or FaceTime him, and he doesn't respond back. Then finally, three days later, he will text back and ask when am I flying to him. I question him on why or what happened I haven't heard from him. His answer is always that he's been busy working. I've noticed that whenever I mention getting extra pay at work, he responds right away.

Annie, maybe, deep down, my heart is saying that maybe he is a scammer and actually doesn't feel about me the way I'd hoped he would.

I get nostalgic looking back on how he treated me four months ago when we first started talking, and it's not the same. I've brought this up with him, but he just insists he's working to make a good life for us when I come.

—*Love Two Men*

DEAR LOVE TWO: In case your heart isn't saying it loudly enough, I'll add my voice to the chorus: This man is a scammer. If that weren't reason enough to lose his number, there's also the fact of your marriage. You and your husband took vows, and that still means something, even if you've grown apart. You owe it to yourselves to try bridging the gulf. Tell him how you're longing for intimacy and affection; commit to marriage counseling together. (There are also online counseling options available, such as BetterHelp and Couples Therapy Inc.)

If you've completely moved on and are going to continue seeing other men, OK, fine. But at least first give your husband the courtesy of a divorce—and don't give new suitors your credit card numbers, passwords, Social Security number, birthdate or other personal data.

Read on for a few additional tips, courtesy of the Federal Bureau of Investigation.

Beware if the individual seems too perfect or quickly asks you to leave a dating service or social media site to communicate directly.

Beware if the individual requests inappropriate photos or financial information.

Beware if the individual promises to meet in person but then always comes up with an excuse why he or she can't. If you haven't met the person after a few months, for whatever reason, you have good reason to be suspicious.

Never send money to anyone you have only communicated with online or by phone.

He's a Toad

DEAR ANNIE: I have never written anything like this before, but I'm beside myself with anger and sadness. My boyfriend of 16 years is leaving me because his two grown children from his marriage do not like me and are refusing to let him see his five grandchildren.

The story goes like this: When we first got together, we were both cheaters. We knew that what we were doing was wrong. Since then, I have never cheated on him.

His wife told their children about his cheating.

We have been living together for the last 2 1/2 years. We were supposed to buy a house together, but then his wife and kids came up with this new plan. My mom had passed away, and he was getting what he wanted—a place in the country where we could live together. He wanted me to put him down as half-owner of the house, but I told him I would only do that after he got a divorce, because if anything were to ever happen to him, I wouldn't pay his wife half of anything that was mine.

He said she wouldn't do that. I told him she would; she had already thrown him under the bus. He wound up buying a house that she found for him. I'm not supposed to know where he lives or even see the place.

He always said that I would be the one who left him, yet he's leaving me in the dust. I feel abandoned and alone. I gave him everything. I got him to go to the best doctors and showed him how to do many things. I did not tell him what to do, yet he's still on a joint phone plan with her. He won't tell me he loves me, because he said he's leaving and it's just not right, but we sleep together and make love. If I ask him whether he loves me, he says yes, but he just won't say it when I need to hear it the most.

I'm so beside myself. I made my life for him and changed everything for him, and now I'm alone and heartbroken. I don't know what to do. I found the one who has my whole heart and soul.

—*Crying Myself to Sleep*

DEAR CRYING MYSELF TO SLEEP: The "one" who has your whole heart and soul would not cheat on his wife with you and continually drag you along. He is trying to have his cake and eat it, too, and he is quite the pig. Stop sleeping with him immediately and tell him it is over. Reach out to family and friends for support while you recover and get over him (and you will; it just might take a little time). Once you find your true prince charming, you will be thrilled that you kicked the toad out of your life.

Husband's Hidden Life

DEAR ANNIE: My second husband and I were together for 20 years. I'll call him "Dominic." We met at a vulnerable time in my life, and he was the kindest man I ever met. Dominic wanted to get married immediately, but I was reluctant, as I'd just gotten out of a marriage with a cheater, liar and abuser.

Dominic begged me. Eventually, I caved. We got married and had a child, my fifth. (I had four from my ex.) Over the years, we had many ups and downs. One day I was getting ready to take a trip and found condoms and lubricant in his duffel bag. When I confronted him about it, he gave me a story. I tried to believe him.

Not long after that, he started buying new clothes and going to the gym. I suspected he had a girlfriend. When I asked what he was up to, he said he couldn't stand my nagging anymore. He moved out. Several months later, he filed for divorce, and during the process had to disclose financial records. That's when I found out he didn't have a girlfriend. He had a boyfriend. I was devastated. When I tried to confront him in arbitration, he wouldn't admit it. It's been four years since then, and I still can't believe it.

I keep thinking back to years back, when we found out our youngest child was gay. I told Dominic that we needed to show her our support, but he refused to even acknowledge the reality. Why would he lie like this? How did I not see it all those years?

—*Still Don't Understand*

DEAR STILL: Don't feel bad for not seeing it. For one, Dominic's dating men now doesn't mean that he was never attracted to you. For another, it sounds as though he was doing everything he could to obfuscate his sexuality even from himself. It saddens me that societal pressures can drive a person so deep into denial. I hope that with time, as we become more accepting, stories like yours will become less common. In supporting your daughter, you're helping to create that brighter future.

Choose and Commit

DEAR ANNIE: I'm so confused, and I don't know what to do. I have been married for four months, and I truly love my husband and believe that he loves me.

My problem is that he cheated on me about two years ago with multiple women, and not only that, he proposed to one of them. It's a long story. But since then, he's been the perfect guy—the person I met six years ago.

I can't seem to get past all the things he did to me before we were married. I cry daily even though it's been two years since it happened. He does everything for me, but I'm very unappreciative. Should I just call it quits and move on? This is the only way I believe I'll get over this. What do you think?

—*Need Answers*

DEAR NEED ANSWERS: The best way to stop agonizing over this is to make a decision and stick with it, no matter what. You could choose to stay with him if you truly believe that he has changed. If so, you must forgive him and put the past in the past—for good. The worst type of suffering we inflict on ourselves is living with resentment and anger. By setting him free, you will set yourself free, too.

On the other hand, if you cannot truly forgive him, you have to break up with him, as living in an ungrateful and angry state will only cause a further divide in your relationship.

You have the power to move on either way. You just have to choose.

Boyfriend Sexting Other Women

How Can I Forgive My Cheating Partner?

DEAR ANNIE: I've been with the same guy for three years. At first, he was incredibly thoughtful and sweet. Over time, I've grown frustrated with how unaffectionate he is. Getting him to express his love feels like trying to wring juice from a dried-out lemon. And he's never introduced me to his family or friends, except for one old friend. Meanwhile, he's met my family and a lot of my friends. Every holiday, he leaves to spend time with his family but doesn't invite me to come with him. Sometimes, I've wondered if he's even really visiting his family.

One day, out of the blue, I received a Facebook message from a girl. She told me that she and my boyfriend had been talking. She showed me all the dirty messages and photos he'd sent her. I couldn't believe it. I was just heartbroken.

That night, I drove to his apartment to get back my house key and left him his things. He confessed that he was talking to another girl but said he has a masturbation addiction; he didn't feel an emotional connection with her. He also insisted that he's never actually been with her sexually.

I was devastated. I thought of just leaving and starting a new relationship. I even downloaded some dating apps. But I really didn't want to give up on the relationship and have tried to stick it out.

It's been hard getting past the cheating. He said that I make him feel bad by bringing up the incident so often. So, for now, we agreed to take space. I still love him so much. And still he keeps calling and texting me. I blocked his number, but I still check the blocked calls folder to see if he's reached out.

I'm just so sad; it's hard to focus on anything. How to move on when I pictured my life with this man? I really want to settle down, and when I did download dating apps, I noticed that the guys on there only seemed to care about one thing, and it wasn't long-term commitment.

—Heart in Shambles

DEAR HEART IN SHAMBLES: End it now, and end it for good. I was ready to tell you that even before I got to the part about his cheating; there's just no good excuse for someone not introducing you to their friends and family after three years. Blocking his number was smart. Now, keep it blocked. Heck, change your number if you need to. Stay busy with friends and hobbies. You can even try dating apps or websites again, just be selective: Some platforms, like Match.com, Hinge or Bumble, have better reputations than others. You will miss him for a time, but once you get over the hump, you'll be so glad you dumped the chump.

Stop Playing Games

DEAR ANNIE: I'm a 34-year-old man with a superb wife. We've been married eight years, and things are great between us. The problem is my mother-in-law. I'm sleeping with her.

She is an incredibly attractive woman and still in her prime. She and my wife look like sisters. But my mother-in-law knows a thing or two more than her daughter in the bedroom.

This affair has been going on for four years now. It's getting hard to not want to be with her all the time, instead of just a couple days a week.

If this should come out, it will wreck two families, and I don't want that. But I think I'm falling or have already fallen in love with my mother-in-law. Plus, the sex is incredible. Any suggestions?

—*My Own Mrs. Robinson*

DEAR MOMR: Get yourself together, man. This isn't advice I should have to give, but please: Stop sleeping with your mother-in-law. Come clean to your wife. And be prepared to pack your bags. As much as I try to encourage married couples to work through thick and thin, honestly, I can't see how someone could come back from this. Your wife deserves to be in a loving, respectful relationship—and not stuck in whatever kind of sick game this is.

Ex Angry I'm Dating

DEAR ANNIE: I am 47 years old. I lost my husband of 23 years two years ago. Since he died, I've dated some men. And last year, I fell for a guy, "Roy." Roy is in his 50s, and he seemed mature at first. I thought he knew what he wanted. He started living at my house and even proposed to me. I thought we'd be planning a wedding. But he changed his routine suddenly, and one week soon after that, he started acting differently. I came to find out that he was talking to other women—exchanging risque Facebook messages and texts. Then I caught him in a hotel with a woman. After that, he stopped talking to me and shacked up with this other woman. He'd never let me know that we had any issues.

A few months after he moved out, he started messaging me again when he was at work or whenever this other woman wasn't around. I wasn't interested in him romantically anymore (I'm seeing someone new), but I thought we could be friends. Finally, I was able to bring him his clothes and stuff, after six months. Well, just this week, he found out I'm with someone, and he gets mad at me. I don't understand that. I've tried being friends, but then he ghosts me after two days of talking. What do you think: Should I cut everything off, or just leave it be? He has lied about us telling people I stole the engagement ring, which is not true.

—*Friend or Faux*

DEAR FRIEND: All good relationships are founded on respect. Roy has not given you any of that—not before as a romantic partner, and not now as a "friend." It's nice to be amicable with exes whenever possible, but for toxic relationships, the healthiest option is usually to cut off all contact. Treat Roy like a biohazard and keep him out of your life, lest he contaminate your current relationship, too.

Unfriended by my Husband

DEAR ANNIE: My husband and I met in high school and have been married for 23 years. Before we were married, we broke up several times and dated other people. He joined Facebook last year, at the end of August. He friended an old girlfriend from high school.

I got mad, and he responded by blocking me. I have never felt the need to check his phone, but something didn't seem right, so I gave in. I checked his phone without his permission. I found out about a week after joining Facebook that he had sent a message to someone he used to work with before we were married, and he asked this person if he knew how to get ahold of an ex-girlfriend he had dated at one of those times when we had broken up.

In the message, he told this person he wanted to see this ex-girlfriend and that he really missed her and has never forgotten her.

I am devastated and not sure what to do. I want to confront him. All these years, I thought we had a good marriage. We have two beautiful teenage children. My heart is broken. I need your advice.

—*Heartbroken*

DEAR HEARTBROKEN: Trust is a fundamental pillar in a marriage, and he has broken that. It is understandable that you are devastated. You and your husband desperately need marriage counseling, whether he admits it or not. If he refuses to go, then tell him what you know about his desire for his old girlfriend and ask him why he is so unhappy in your marriage.

Ideally, you can confront him about his text messages with a counselor in the session so there will be a moderator in what is likely to be a heated exchange—with the goal being to get your marriage back on track. He has to stop bullying you by doing things like blocking you on Facebook. You are supposed to be on the same team.

Stop Putting Up with a Cheater

DEAR ANNIE: I met a man about four years ago. We started dating a week after we met, upon his insistence. Well, after we were together a year, I found out that he was messaging with a girl online and had been for several months. She didn't want him. Then, a month after that, I heard he cheated on me with someone from work who was in her early 20s, the same age as his daughter. I confronted him, but he refused to admit he was guilty. However, I've caught him exchanging sexual messages with a couple of other girls online since then. He says he's never actually hooked up with them in person.

I guess my question for you is, is it worth trying to keep this man in my life? I love him, and he says he loves me, but part of me is no longer in love with him. If I'm being honest, I've felt this way ever since I heard of his cheating with that young woman. What do you think, Annie: Should I set him on the curb on trash day? My heart is telling me to stay, but my mind is wanting me to tell him to get lost.

—*Confused Girlfriend*

DEAR CONFUSED: Listen to your mind on this one. Not only did he cheat on you more than once (the racy messages count as cheating), but he's also shown no interest in truly making it right by you. Life is short, and your time is too precious to squander on someone who doesn't value it. While at first it might feel hard to live without him, eventually, you'll look back and wonder how you lived with him for as long as you did.

Let Her Go

DEAR ANNIE: I am a man in my late 50s. Until recently, I was in a long-distance relationship with a woman—let's call her "Maria"—who lives about a thousand miles away from me. Last month, out of the blue, she accused me of cheating on her with her cousin, who lives about 45 minutes away from me. This is 100% not true. I met the cousin only once, when Maria was in town for a visit last year. I have not seen or communicated with her cousin since!

Because of these accusations and Maria's insistence that she is right, sadly, we have split. I love Maria, and I have always told her that and showed her in every way I could. We haven't talked in weeks, since our conversations kept ending in arguments. She says she has "proof," which she has yet to show. She absolutely cannot have proof, because it didn't happen! But how do I prove that something did not happen? Maria and I talked or texted every night, and I told her to call me or video chat me anytime to show I was alone at night. In past relationships, Maria has had trust issues and cheating partners, so I'm thinking that might be where this is coming from. Is there any hope?

—*Wrongfully Accused*

DEAR WRONGFULLY ACCUSED: I see two possibilities here. Option A: Maria was looking for an excuse to end the relationship, so she invented one. Option B: She truly believes that you cheated on her, despite your giving her no reason to believe such a thing. Either way, my advice is to let her go. A loving partner doesn't make baseless, hurtful accusations.

To Tell or Not

DEAR ANNIE: To "My Own Mrs. Robinson," who said his marriage was great and the problem was his mother-in-law, with whom he was sleeping: Your mother-in-law isn't the problem. It's your shameful lack of honor and morals. The humiliation your young wife is about to experience will likely last a lifetime and this is exactly what you wanted since sex was more important to you than the devastating harm you were willing to inflict.

To the young wife:

1. This is not your fault.

2. Immediately contact a divorce attorney.

3. If OKed by the attorney, change the locks on the house and put his belongings on the front sidewalk.

4. Immediately divorce this pathetic excuse of a man and never look back.

5. Say no more than five words to your disgraceful mother: "Do not ever contact me again." How I wish I could put my arms around this young wife and comfort her.

—K.S.

DEAR K.S.: A lot of people wrote in about that letter, with a few suggesting that "MOMR" must have been pulling my leg because it was so outrageous. I really hope so. Otherwise, that poor wife is about to be handed a lifetime's worth of baggage. Thanks for your letter.

Endless Chain of Cheating

DEAR ANNIE: The guy I've been seeing for five years has been seeing a married woman for 18 years. For context, we're all seniors. He's in his 80s; I'm in my 70s. The married woman is in her 60s.

The two of them have gone on road trips all over the country, visiting all 48 of the contiguous states in the country. Her husband has apparently been clueless this whole time, always thinking she's traveling with some girlfriend.

My boyfriend says he loves me more than her and that it will never truly work with her since they can't live together. But their relationship interferes with ours. She's even come to his house when I've been there. (He wouldn't let her in, and she slapped him across both cheeks.) What should I do? I don't want to waste time on a loser.

—*Impatiently Waiting*

DEAR IMPATIENTLY: There's so much cheating going on here that it's hard to keep track. The worst part is that you're cheating yourself out of a caring relationship by sticking around for this two-timer. Break the chain of fools and free yourself up for better things, such as new hobbies, family, friends—and men without married girlfriends.

When to Move in Together

DEAR ANNIE: Recently, I left my husband of 17 years. He always had a problem being happy with just one woman, and he cheated on me multiple times. Mostly, I was able to push past it. But a couple of months ago, I learned that he slept with my only full-blooded sister 10 years ago. That was the last straw. I filed for divorce.

Since then, I've started seeing a longtime close friend. He works a lot, so we haven't been able to spend too much time together in person, but we talk on the phone every day, sometimes for four, five, even six hours. And when we are together, I feel wanted. I can see and feel the love in the way that he looks at me. We can sit around for hours, just cuddling and looking into each other's eyes. I've seen things like this in the movies but never imagined I'd have it in my life! I'd always disregarded the idea of soul mates, but now I truly feel that I have found mine.

Although we've only been dating a couple of months, we've been friends for more than a decade. We watched each other's kids grow up. We've been there for each other through relationship issues and divorces (his and now mine). My question to you: When would it be wise for us to move in with each other? Every time we are together, it's getting so much harder for us to say goodbye. We live pretty far apart and both have busy work schedules, so we are always stretched for time. We have discussed the possibility of living together but agreed we do not want to ruin this amazing thing we have going by rushing. But how long do we have to wait?

—*Head Over Heels*

DEAR HEAD OVER HEELS: While you've known each other as friends for quite some time, you're still just barely acquainted as lovers, and that's different. Give it another six months or so, until your divorce is finalized and those butterflies in your stomach have settled a bit. Take time to understand how the other person works. See what happens when an argument or conflict arises: How does he handle it? Are you able to talk through it calmly together? Knowing these things upfront—ensuring a solid foundation—will help you two build a strong relationship that stands the test of time.

Don't Go Crawling Back

DEAR ANNIE: My 67-year-old boyfriend of 12 years threw me out for a 22-year-old, but soon afterward, he called and said he thought we could still work it out. We ran into each other in public a month ago, and he couldn't keep his hands off me. He said he'd call me that night, but he never did. And when I tried him, he didn't pick up. He later sent me a text saying: "Not gonna happen. Too late." I have a feeling that he won't speak to me or see me because he knows that he'll want me back.

Right now, all my belongings are still at his place. I told him that once they leave, they won't come back. He has said nothing to me about getting my stuff, but I'm going to just show up. I still love him deeply and want to try to make this work. What have I got to lose?

—*Pining for Him*

DEAR PINING: A better question is, what do you have to gain by continuing to give your heart to someone who keeps tossing it aside? It's time you drop him like a bad habit. The longer you go without seeing him, the easier it will get and the healthier you will become. If you don't think you'll be able to resist his charms when retrieving your stuff, ask a friend or family member to go. Stay strong.

Best Friend Turned Cheating Boyfriend

DEAR ANNIE: My longtime best friend of 15 years and I entered into a romantic relationship in March of last year. It was a nightmare from almost the very beginning. There were faults and failures on both sides, but ultimately, it ended when it came to light that he had not only been cheating on me but also gotten the other girl pregnant!

The breakup has left me very confused and deeply hurt and traumatized. I miss my best friend more than anything. We've had no contact for more than a month now, but lately the urge to reach out to him has been overwhelming. What do I do? Is it better to leave things as they stand? Is reaching out a bad idea?

—Missing My Best Friend

DEAR MMBF: Wounds can get itchy when they're healing. That doesn't mean we should scratch them. The longing you feel to talk to your ex right now is an itch that shouldn't be scratched. Take time to mend and focus on your own mental health and personal development. Try new hobbies. Establish positive routines. When you feel yourself wanting to reach out to him, reach out to another friend instead. It won't be easy, but it will get a little bit easier every day.

Delusions of Infidelity

DEAR ANNIE: Your response to "Wrongfully Accused," the man in the long-distance relationship with a woman who wrongly accuses him of infidelity, misses another possibility. She may have a paranoid delusional disorder known as Othello syndrome. Those diagnosed with it are unable to distinguish between reality and their delusions that a spouse or partner is being unfaithful. My wife of 35 years is continually tormented by these thoughts, and it causes great stress in our marriage. But I would never leave her.

—Faithful Husband

DEAR FAITHFUL HUSBAND: Until receiving your letter, I had never heard of Othello syndrome, which is "a psychotic disorder characterized by delusion of infidelity or jealousy," as noted in the Journal of Psychiatry and Clinical Neurosciences in 2012. Although it's a rare condition, it's a possibility worth considering, for sure. Thank you for writing.

Gaining Pleasure Elsewhere

DEAR ANNIE: I'm desperately in need of your advice. I've been married to my husband for 16 years; we've been together 20 years. We'd always had a decent sex life up until two years ago. The sex just stopped. He was never in the mood. I had no clue what had changed. Well, about six months ago, I discovered that he's been watching porn a couple of times a week (at least), for as far back as our computer history showed. I confronted him about it. He said it was no big deal—that most men have a porn habit. But it is a big deal to me. It has lowered my self-esteem and made me feel very lonely and unlovable—like it's my fault that he doesn't want me.

He acts like I should be OK with it, but to me, what he's doing is a form of cheating. I don't know what to do or how to handle it.

—Feeling Betrayed

DEAR FEELING: If this were indeed just a habit, then there might be middle ground on which to meet him. But when a behavior becomes so compulsive that it disrupts one's marriage and prevents physical intimacy for years on end, it's no longer a habit. It's an addiction.

Have a heart-to-heart with your husband. While your hurt feelings are understandable, try to set aside any anger when you talk to him about this. Put love front and center, expressing concern for his health and letting him know how his behavior impacts you. Hopefully, he'll be open to seeking help overcoming this addiction, through counseling or a support group. Regardless, you can seek help for yourself. Visit https://www.psychologytoday.com/groups/sexual-addiction, and enter your ZIP code to find groups for those addicted to pornography as well as groups for spouses/partners.

Marriage Takes Two

DEAR ANNIE: I have been married to my wife for just over two years. We each have a child from a previous marriage, and we have a child together. A few months ago, she started accusing me of distancing myself from her. I was confused by this, as I truly hadn't intended to. I thought everything had been going OK.

Well, it turns out that she was the one trying to distance herself. She told me last month that she wants to take some time apart to figure out if she still wants to be with me.

I've tried talking to her about it to find out why she wants space. She's given me a variety of different reasons. I've heard her out, acknowledged her concerns and offered solutions—but they're never enough. She just comes up with more excuses. She has also mentioned that men flirt with her at work and she enjoys the attention.

She says she's still making up her mind about our marriage, but I feel like I can read the writing on the wall and know where this is headed. I'm absolutely heartbroken. Any advice you could offer would be absolutely welcome.

—*So Very Lost*

DEAR LOST: Marriages can survive almost anything if both partners are willing to put in the work. But your wife isn't meeting you halfway, or even part of the way. In fact, she seems intent on heading the opposite direction. Keep focusing on what you can control, and if she ultimately decides she wants out, know that you did all you could. By the sound of it, you're a loving, caring partner, and if your wife can't appreciate that, someone else will, down the line. But I am sorry for your heartache in the meantime.

Dating My Ex-Husband

DEAR ANNIE: I've been in a relationship with my boyfriend for about two years. He's actually my ex-husband from 25 years ago, and we reunited about 16 months ago. We do not live together, but he's made it clear that he wants to move in that direction and even hints that we should remarry. However, last March, we had a serious falling out and were broken up for about three weeks. During our break, he met a woman, "Rachel," on a dating app, and they went to lunch a few times. After my boyfriend and I reunited, he continued to meet with Rachel on coffee dates and walks along the beach near her home. I expressed to him that I did not like the situation because they met on a dating app, even though he claims there is no sexual or romantic interest between them. He says he just enjoys her company, that she's a really "cool person" and that they both have grown kids and things in common.

We've now had a few arguments about the subject, and it's causing tension. He says I "can't have it both ways" because I have a couple of male friends, too, and he has no problem with my relationships with them. But my male friends have been in my life for decades, and there has never been anything sexual or romantic with either of these men. Also, he talks with Rachel every week, and I only ever see my male friends about once or twice a year. This just doesn't feel good, and I don't know how to handle it. I'm afraid to even broach the subject again because he gets very upset. I love reading your column and could really use some advice. I'm not an insecure person by nature, but I feel really uncomfortable with this. Am I just being petty and possessive?

—*Am I Petty?*

DEAR AIP: It's entirely reasonable for you to feel uncomfortable with your boyfriend taking walks on the beach with a woman he met on a dating app. It's noteworthy that he was on dating apps at all, when you were only broken up for three weeks. And it's concerning that he's brushed away your feelings about the matter so flippantly.

You and your ex have a lot of history together, which can be a liability when it comes to clearly assessing a situation. I'd encourage you to take a step back from this relationship and evaluate how you're feeling, in your gut and in your heart.

Gone Goodbye

DEAR ANNIE: My significant other and I were in a relationship for 15 years. One evening, I was feeling insecure and asked whether there was someone else. Very soon after that, my significant other completely cut off all contact with me.

We were in a commitment and planning to get married, but now there is absolutely no communication, which just drives me to want to contact him even more than I would have in the past.

I'm trying to stay anchored in optimism, hoping that this storm will pass, he will get back in touch and we will restore our relationship.

How does a person shut down and not have any communication? This has spurred me to start obsessing. Without the ability to know when we will speak again, I feel paralyzed. It's very irritating, and it makes me feel totally separate from this person.

Wouldn't it create a better outcome if there were a resounding "no" or if we talked it through? How long do I hold on? Maybe it's too late. Or maybe even if he were to come back, I should be wary and concerned that he could have ever completely shut down like this. Thanks in advance for your input.

—*Left Behind*

DEAR LEFT: People often live in a state of open-ended anguish when a loved one goes missing or dies in a way that makes a body irretrievable. Denial is a stage of grief, and without concrete evidence of a person's death, it can be very hard to move past it.

Similarly, without a definite breakup from your partner, you're stuck in a holding pattern. That's what makes his cowardly behavior so unbelievably cruel and selfish.

If he has made himself totally unreachable, then you need to decide once and for all that things are over between you. Truly over. Only then can you have closure, properly mourn the relationship and move on.

Whatever you do, don't blame yourself. One moment of your feeling insecure should not lead your significant other to cut off all ties after being in a relationship for 15 years. I would ask what prompted your suspicions in the first place. Trust your intuition.

Annie Lane

Giving Up on Dating

DEAR ANNIE: I want to know why people think it's OK to harass and abuse other people. My ex brought his girlfriend home, and they spent the night in the garage. That was when we were still married.

Then he took my 5-year-old daughter out on dates with the girlfriend, and he abused and harassed me for a year to try to get me to abandon the house and my daughter so he wouldn't have to pay child support.

During this ordeal, I was ripped off by a lawyer who knew my ex was harassing me and did nothing. My ex and the girl are not together anymore, but I later found out that the girlfriend was hitting my daughter on her hands to punish her when she did something wrong.

I just don't get why there are horrible people in the world who do awful things and don't think they've done anything wrong. It is not unusual for them to turn the situation on you, acting as if you deserved it.

After all this, I'm done with men. I don't even date. It ain't worth it. I talk to people on chat sites, and they tell me they don't date for the same reasons. Being alone in this day and age is just the better way to go. I feel so broken and empty inside; no one would want me anyway. I am ruined, and no one seems to care.

So, I just want to know—why?!

—Someone Who Just Wants to Know Why

DEAR KNOW WHY: Hurt people hurt people. Whether they were hurt when they were children and are repeating the same patterns or they were hurt when they were adults—it doesn't matter where the meanness came from. Being cruel to other human beings never feels good in the long run.

I'm not sure that making blanket statements, such as saying that you are finished with dating forever, is going to make you feel better in the long run. Just commit to only surrounding yourself with people who lift you up and have your best interests at heart. I would also let your ex know that his ex-girlfriend is never allowed to be around your daughter again. Child abuse is a serious crime and needs to be treated as such.

Cheating in the Chatroom

DEAR ANNIE: My husband and I have been married for five years. We have a beautiful daughter, and we've got a son on the way. But I keep finding my husband using dating websites and chatrooms for singles. When I ask him about it, he gets angry and says, "That's from months ago!" But whenever I check the browser history, there are always more recently visited websites. He says that he never talks to anyone, just looks. How can I make him see that I love him and that those are not sites for married people? Should I just give up and end the marriage? I'm at a loss.

—Taken for Granted

DEAR TAKEN: You don't need to make him see that those sites aren't for married people. He already knows. He just doesn't care or is too addicted to the rush to stop. Whatever the case, his blatant disregard for your feelings is shocking, and the fact that he's doing all this while you're pregnant adds insult to injury. If you two are going to truly work through this, it will be with the help of a marriage counselor. If he refuses to go, then it might be time to start speaking discreetly with an attorney about your options.

Annie Lane

Love Versus Lust

DEAR ANNIE: I've known this guy "Henry" for about six years now. We never got the timing right, and we've cheated on our significant others with each other. When I was single, he wasn't, and vice versa. Now I'm in a healthy and happy relationship. Henry and I still talk, and it's hard to let him go. He's had trouble letting me go, too.

I used to believe I was in love with him, and I still have feelings for him. His attitude has changed during the past year. He's been real sweet and asks me what I want in the future. We both want the same things out of life. We share similar interests and get along very well. He makes me feel a different way than any other man has. He has asked me to run away with him and start a life together in a new state. I don't know if he would actually go through with it. He's very spontaneous but also flaky.

However, my current boyfriend, "Mason," has been there for me through a crazy and tough time. Mason is real sweet, too, and he's helped me grow a lot as a person. He lives with me, and we want the same things out of life. Mason would do anything for me to make sure I'm happy in the relationship. We communicate well and haven't had any issues yet.

I don't want to make a stupid choice and regret everything. If I leave Mason, I don't think there's any going back. But I worry I'll always wonder what could have been with Henry.

—*Love Dilemma in Vermont*

DEAR DILEMMA: I'm not sure how happy and healthy your current relationship is if you are still lusting for Henry. Ask yourself if what you are feeling is more lust or love for Henry—and Mason—and that will give you your answer.

Lust dissipates over time, while love persists. Whether Henry or Mason is more love or lust is a question you have to ask yourself. Start by asking, "How do I feel about myself when I am with this person?" Don't forget that if Henry cheated on others, he will likely cheat on you.

Regaining Trust Takes Time

DEAR ANNIE: I love reading your column. I found out three years ago that my husband of 33 years was having an affair with his bookkeeper. We have a business together, but I stepped out of the business part years ago to become a nurse.

Supposedly, the affair has ended, but he refuses to let her stop being his bookkeeper. It's been three long years of wondering. I have no idea about the financial part of the business.

My heart breaks because we have been together since high school, but I can't continue to have all these doubts. Any suggestions without tearing my world apart?

—*Heartbroken*

DEAR HEARTBROKEN: Doubting and not knowing for sure is one of the most difficult positions to be in. It's better to know for sure than to constantly doubt. What your husband did made you lose your trust, and once trust is gone from a relationship, it takes a lot of steps to regain that. Keeping the woman who he had an affair with employed is unacceptable. You have every right to feel heartbroken, but know that you will heal from this. Consult the help of a professional therapist to help you deal with the betrayal of your husband. From there, you can decide if YOU want to stay with him and what YOUR terms are for keeping this relationship going.

Once a decision is made, you will start to feel better and heal from the trauma that you suffered.

Husband Has a Wandering Eye

DEAR ANNIE: My husband and I are both in our mid-60s and retired. He has a habit that is really starting to irk and hurt me the last few years. When we're out together and he sees attractive women, he always looks twice at them. He apologizes but then, after a couple of weeks, does it again! I have told him, repeatedly, that it is disrespectful and that if I don't do it for him anymore, he should go get what he is looking for—but that he shouldn't expect to be able to come back afterward. He says that I'm jealous and immature. I say that he should know better. What do you say?

—Weary of Watching Him Watch Them

DEAR WEARY: Leering is one thing; just looking is another. If your husband is merely taking quick second glances at women, let it go. It's normal—healthy, even—to take momentary notice of attractive people. It doesn't mean he finds you any less attractive. As long as he's being faithful to you, physically and emotionally, that's what matters.

How Can I Forgive My Cheating Partner?

How Do I Make It Right After Cheating on my Boyfriend?

DEAR ANNIE: My boyfriend and I have been together for six years now. Two years ago, I cheated on him, and he found out shortly after when he looked at my phone and saw that I was texting the other guy. At the time, I panicked and said that my best friend, "Deb," had been using my phone. I then reached out to Deb and begged her to cover for me and lie if my boyfriend asked her about it. She did, and he bought the excuse. But a few weeks later, I confessed the truth to him, including the fact that Deb had covered up for me. We've been trying to work past this ever since. I feel awful about my infidelity. It has affected me in ways I never thought it would, just as I know it's affected him very deeply, too. It worsened my depression and anxiety.

On top of the shame I feel for cheating, I have been unable to spend as much time as I'd like with Deb. My boyfriend wants nothing to do with her. Anytime she comes up in conversation, he says that she's fake or a liar. He refuses to hang out with her. This woman has been my best friend for 23 years, and she's very important to me. But he hates it when I spend time with her.

I know that this is all my fault. Annie, what can I do to make it right?

—*Regretful Girlfriend*

DEAR REGRETFUL: It sounds as though your boyfriend has some unresolved feelings over your cheating and he's taking them out on your friend. If you really care about each other, enlist the help of a couples therapist to work through these issues in a healthy way. Otherwise, you'll forever feel guilty; he'll forever feel angry; and the two of you will rack up toxic levels of resentment.

A Promiscuous Former Life

DEAR ANNIE: My wife and I have been together since we were just out of high school. We've been married for 18 years, and we have three glorious children. We have a great relationship, but I recently discovered she was extremely promiscuous in high school and found out she slept with many of our friends, some of whom are still in our social circle. I have always had a jealous nature, and now the jealousy is overwhelming my daily thoughts, especially when we see these other guys. Although the encounters happened before my time with her, I still feel cheated on and don't look at her the way I once did. I have not brought it up with her, because I know she will get super defensive, and I know she will not go to counseling because of the nature of the topic. Any insight into getting over this would be appreciated, as I do love her and want to be with her.

—Jealous in Wisconsin

DEAR JEALOUS: Your wife is still looking at you with the same love in her eyes she always has, and if she knew you now look at her differently because of things she did 20 years ago, she would be heartbroken. So don't tell her. Though I generally champion the importance of talking every problem out with a romantic partner, unfounded jealousy is the exception. If you aired your feelings, they'd grow like fanned flames. You'd most likely make your wife feel defensive, and her defensiveness would in turn make you feel less secure about the marriage. Deprive these fiery feelings of oxygen and they'll eventually die out.

It's also not worth talking about it with her because this is about you, not your relationship. Do some digging and try to get to the root of your insecurity. Use positive self-talk to encourage rational thinking. And if the obsessive thoughts won't stop nagging you, consider therapy.

Hung Up Over a Stupid Comment

DEAR ANNIE: My husband and I own a boat that takes tourists on short trips. Three years ago, he fell in love with the only woman on board. When I realized something was up, I said, "If she is so wonderful, what is stopping you from being with her?" Without hesitation, he said, "The age difference."

I have not been able to stop thinking about that every day for the past three years. I am becoming upset even writing this to you. She is not interested in him. I guess he is old enough to be her father. But what if he meets someone his own age? I think I'd better see my lawyer. What do you think? Should we get a divorce?

—*Seasick*

DEAR SEASICK: I can't tell you whether you should get a divorce based on your letter. But I can tell you that you can't keep living this way. One comment has been eating away at you for three years, and you need to put a stop to that before it swallows you whole. Have you tried talking to your husband? It's possible his comment was a joke, albeit a mean one. In any case, I'd strongly recommend a few sessions of marriage counseling so you can open up the lines of communication.

Annie Lane

Solve Your Own Relationship Issues

DEAR ANNIE: My wife "Monica" has been having a mostly texting affair with "Mike" for almost two years. There are emails where they address each other with, "Hey, babe." It is disgusting. I accidentally discovered this years ago, and again recently after I thought they had not talked for years.

Upon this discovery, I texted Mike angrily—he is not someone I actually know, but I took his number from my wife's phone—and my wife claims that it's "over." I've heard this before.

My wife asked me not to contact Mike's wife because "they would probably divorce if she found out." Why would I care about that? My wife thinks Mike is "a friend" and wouldn't want to see him hurt. I am sure he's not "a friend" and obviously wants something more.

Why should I honor my wife's wishes here? Doesn't Mike's wife deserve to know that he's in love with another woman? (His words, expressed in an email.)

Why do I have to be the only person who knows about this situation? I feel like someone else knowing—Mike's wife, or maybe my wife's mom—might shock either of these two people into realizing that they are risking too much by carrying on this way. We have kids, as do Mike and his wife.

Why shouldn't I tell Mike's wife? Doesn't she have a right to know about her husband's infidelity?

—*Let the Truth Out*

DEAR LET THE TRUTH OUT: Yes, Mike's wife has a right to know about her husband's infidelity—if, in fact, he has been unfaithful to her. Mike has to be the one to tell her about his feelings for your wife instead of you. Rather than focusing on someone else's relationship, continue to focus on your own.

Seek marriage counseling with your wife. Try to understand why she needs an emotional connection with another man via texting instead of you. Maybe you will learn something. I know you are hurting about the texts you found—and I am sorry for that—but hurting Mike's wife will not make it better. Instead, focus on repairing your relationship. Let Mike figure out his own stuff. When we lie to the ones we love, we only hurt ourselves, so my guess is that Mike is already suffering. Best of luck to you and your wife.

Is My Relationship Doomed?

DEAR ANNIE: My boyfriend and I have been in a relationship for 10 years. We've had a lot of trials but always managed to hold onto each other and weather the storms. The last major trial was that I cheated on him with one of our best friends. I feel terrible about it; in fact, I think I may have managed to break my heart more than my boyfriend's. Anyway, he says that he still loves me, and we're still together. But we no longer share a bed; we no longer share much of anything, honestly, except a roof and a rare romantic night now and then. Should I let him go or just give him more time to truly forgive me? I love this man beyond measure, but if I'm destined to be hurt, I'd like to just get it over with now.

—Guilt-Ridden Boyfriend

DEAR GUILT-RIDDEN: Betrayal hurts. Sometimes it inflicts wounds too deep for either partner to adequately treat on his or her own, no matter how badly they want to make it better. A couples therapist can help you begin the real healing. Make an appointment today.

Jealousy Isn't Healthy

DEAR ANNIE: I am a woman in my mid-30s, and my wife is in her early 40s. We met a little less than two years ago and haven't left each other's side since. We got married about a year ago. Needless to say, we both fell fast and hard for each other. When I met her, my whole world changed, and I look at the world in a completely different way. She makes me want to be a better person altogether. But we have a problem. My wife already had trust issues from a previous relationship in which she was betrayed. Well, several months ago, I broke her trust by talking to my ex on the phone. It was an innocent conversation, but I knew that it would upset my wife. I felt terrible and immediately admitted what I'd done, admitted that it was wrong and promised that it wouldn't ever happen again.

Fast-forward four months, and nothing seems to be enough for my wife. She continues to throw it in my face. Every time my phone makes a noise, she wants to look at it. There's not a day that goes by that she doesn't make a smart-aleck remark about my talking to my ex on the phone. I am truly lost because I love this woman more than life itself and have never been happier. But I can't continue to allow her to say the mean and hurtful things she's been saying, and I can't take the distance between us, and I can't take any more of the barrages of questions. I love her and don't want to ever face life without her, but the cruelty is breaking me down quickly. I don't know what to do anymore.

—*Heartbroken Wife*

DEAR HEARTBROKEN: Jealous, controlling behavior is not the stuff of a healthy relationship, and it can veer into emotionally abusive territory. Your wife's past relationship issues don't give her license to treat you poorly. You love her and want her in your life—but she needs to seek individual counseling and/or to attend couples counseling with you so that you can both have a shot at a healthy, sustainable life together built on trust.

Boyfriend Is Hiding Things

DEAR ANNIE: My boyfriend and I have been dating for two years. He's a hard worker, which appealed to me, as I've always been the breadwinner in previous relationships. But lately, I feel like he's not putting any effort into the relationship.

For one, we always hang out at my house. I've only been to his house three times in the two years we've been dating. For another, he does not allow me on his social media. He refuses to accept my friend requests, and he never posts any photos of me.

We used to see each other once a week, but lately he's been working so much that we only see each other once a month. I get that he's busy, but it's starting to seem like he really doesn't care whether he sees me or not. I confronted him about this, and he got upset and accused me of trying to stir up drama. I'm not trying to stir up drama; I just don't want to go through this anymore. When I told him as much, he hung up on me. Apparently, it's annoying to him when I share my feelings. As his girlfriend, I expect to see him more than once a month. We only live 20 minutes apart! I'm just not satisfied with the level of attention I'm getting in this relationship at this point. He does frequently tell me that he loves me, and he calls me every day. But I sometimes feel like I'm an afterthought. What is your opinion on this?

—*Back-Burnered*

DEAR BACK-BURNERED: It sounds like he's got another pot on the stove. And if he's not cheating on you, he might as well be. Only seeing you once a month, never having you over to his place, excluding you from his social media—of course you're not satisfied. He's feeding you scraps. You deserve to be with someone who makes you a proud part of his life. The sooner you end things with him, the sooner you open yourself up to bigger and better things.

Sudden Change in Tone

DEAR ANNIE: I got back with my ex after two years of separation. We have a beautiful baby girl together, and I really love this lady. When I suggested marriage, she was happy and looking forward to it; however, out of the blue, she changed her mind and even asked for space. She told me that I should start calling her before I go to visit her and our girl.

This really confused me, and I even started suspecting she was seeing someone else. This has really affected me greatly, and I don't know if I should even go ahead with the marriage anymore.

Kindly advise; am I being unrealistic and selfish?

—*Confused*

DEAR CONFUSED: No, I don't think you are being unrealistic or selfish at all. I think you are confused and hurt. And for good reason. A complete change in attitude in any relationship is a red flag that something is not right. The best way to figure out what is going on is to tell her how you feel and ask her why her behavior toward you has shifted so dramatically.

Husband's Eyes Are Always on the Move

DEAR ANNIE: My husband and I have been together for 28 years. He's a very sweet and loving man, but his watching other women really bothers me. It happens whenever we're out together, even in church!

I know there will always be women who are better-looking or better built; but it's really demeaning and leaves me with such an empty feeling. I've talked to him about this, and he doesn't seem to take my concerns seriously. A simple glance, not a problem, but to continue watching is just too much.

What do I do? Do I keep smiling and pretend not to notice? What can I do? At this point, I don't like going out.

—*Feeling Insignificant in Florida*

DEAR FEELING INSIGNIFICANT: On a positive note, wandering eyes are better than wandering hands. I am glad that you aren't concerned that something more serious is happening, which implies that the foundation of your marriage is strong.

Given that, you should be able to have a direct conversation with your husband. Let him know that this makes you feel insignificant to him and that it hurts. Understand that he will likely continue to notice attractive people but that he shouldn't look more than a simple glance. Offer to come up with a cue that will recall his attention if he lapses, such as a tug at his hand. It will likely take a bit of training because he probably isn't aware that he's even staring.

Fifty Years Unforgiven

DEAR ANNIE: For close to 50 years, my friend "Chloe" and I have met for dinner once a week, and she always discusses her husband's past affair, which occurred over 50 years ago and lasted a year. They are still married and had a few children after the affair ended. She seems to refuse to believe he has told her "everything" and still asks him questions about it.

I empathize with her pain and repeatedly tell her that forgiveness is about her being happy again within herself and that it does not mean she condones her husband's past behavior. She has been very mean to him all these years and says hateful things to him, which distresses their daughters.

They have been to couples therapy a few times, but nothing has changed with her. I am at a loss to figure out why she keeps this up after all these years. I need some understanding of why she repeatedly expresses hate for her husband but continues to live with him. Does she need to be a victim?

—*Concerned and Confused*

DEAR CC: You are a good friend with wise advice, and Chloe is lucky to have you on the receiving end of her weekly pity parties.

It sounds like Chloe is using a "victim mentality" to avoid dealing with deeper relationship problems. If she forgives her husband's infidelity, she'll have to assume some responsibility for the failures in her marriage. It's far easier to just lay the blame on him.

Still, it is clear she has some unresolved feelings of rejection. Fifty years is a long time to be carrying around so much anger, and she must be tired. Chloe has two options here: leave her husband, or forgive him.

If she chooses to forgive, remind her once more that forgiveness is not a stamp of approval for his actions; it is merely an acknowledgement that their marriage and their family are more important than a mistake he made 50 years ago.

Knowledge Is Power

DEAR ANNIE: This is in response to "Let the Truth Out." I was the woman on the hurt partner end of an affair, and I disagree with your advice not to tell the wife about her husband's cheating. The cheater informing their spouse is something that rarely happens, which perpetuates the lie.

In the end, someone outside the marriage should inform the hurt partner. Hurt partners not knowing about infidelity stifles opportunities for the couple to seek support and does not afford opportunity for partners to move forward.

My husband cheated on me 20 years ago. The affair came to light recently, after 41 years of marriage. Only now, with the help of a counselor, are we dealing with the hurt, pain and destruction that this long-kept deception caused, and we are finally repairing issues in our marriage.

My husband's affair was with a person with whom he worked. Knowing that the school staff knew and gossiped about the two of them, and it was public knowledge within our community, is extraordinarily hurtful. The fact that no one told me allowed the affair to continue for 14 months. If I had known about the affair when it was going on, it might have ended earlier, and we could have dealt with issues in our marriage 20 years sooner.

Yes, it could have ended in divorce, but at least I wouldn't have been living in a marriage that was a sham for 20 years and could have been with someone deserving of my love. I contend that telling the hurt partner is hurtful but not cruel. In the end, someone informing the hurt partner allows opportunity for healing or for the marriage to be terminated. The real cruelty to the hurt partner is living a lie.

Finding out about an affair is devastating, but when the hurt partner is made aware of the deception, the couple has an opportunity to deal with issues in their marriage. No matter what choices are made regarding the marriage, the hurt partner is not living in an unfulfilling marriage fraught with deception. Knowing is a gift.

—*Wishing I Would Have Known*

DEAR WISHING: Thank you for your letter, and I hope you and your husband find healing through the truth. If you love him, work on forgiving him, for your sake. Remember the old saying that acid can do more damage to the vessel in which it is stored than to anything on which it is poured.

Gawking Husband Is Taught a Lesson

DEAR ANNIE: My husband used to check out other women in an obvious way, but no more.

What happened was this: We were in our early 40s, both on our second marriages, and we met for a date one night after work. We sat at the bar due to the crowd on a Friday, and two women across the bar were flirting with him. Just smiles and eye games, but he was soaking up the attention, essentially ignoring me.

I quietly got up, took my purse, walked out and drove home. It took him a minute to realize that I was gone, and those women were cracking up!

He came home just a few minutes behind me, all embarrassed because I had ditched him. I let him know that I didn't care if he appreciated pretty women but gawking in my presence was flat-out disrespectful. It never happened again.

—*Expecting Respect*

DEAR EXPECTING RESPECT: Thank you for sharing your very creative way to get your husband to stop gawking at other women. Most times, people treat us the way we expect to be treated. Good for you.

Age Gap Is Inappropriate

DEAR ANNIE: My husband is 59 years old and thinks it is OK to ogle young girls less than 18 years of age—more like 15 to 16. He does this with me present and says it is natural behavior and that all men do it.

I say it is disrespectful to me and resembles pedophile behavior. I am 64 years old, and he had an affair with a 29-year-old female about a year ago. What is your opinion?

—*Feeling the Sting of Growing Old*

DEAR GROWING OLD: I'm not sure why your husband's actions are making you feel old instead of disgusted. You should dump him. His pedophile behavior—and, yes, that is what it is—has nothing to do with your age and everything to do with his Lolita complex. He needs to seek treatment immediately. A 59-year-old man staring at 15-year-old girls and having an affair with a girl in her 20s? You can do better.

Friends Need to Speak Up About Infidelity

DEAR ANNIE: I was married for 10 years to the father of my 40-year-old daughter. We divorced when she was 7; he left me to continue a relationship I didn't know he was having. That lasted six months. He has since been married twice more and had many other relationships between and during those marriages. The thing is, I had no idea he was not monogamous until he left.

I have always been well-employed and capable of supporting myself and our daughter without a second income. Before he left me, he took a distant job that uprooted me, with my compliance, because we were married and, I thought, happy. We moved again, and I went along.

How Can I Forgive My Cheating Partner?

Less than a month after he left me, several longtime friends told me they knew of his affairs before our daughter was born. My point: People in a relationship, or who think they're in a relationship, with a player deserve to know about it as soon as their friends do. I would never have temporarily short-circuited my career, left my home city, or packed and unpacked households endlessly had I known about his predilections. Thank goodness he left when he did!

It's been 33 years. My daughter and I are close; I have a great life and career. But I'm weighing in because of the queasiness I read here on this subject; just like you'd tell a friend that she has spinach in her teeth or toilet paper on her shoe, for heaven's sake, give her a heads up if you're certain that her spouse repeatedly acts single when she's not around.

To answer an unspoken question, I never felt angry at my friends. Enough time was already wasted.

—*The Truth Set Me Free*

DEAR TRUTH: It sounds like you made great steps toward creating a wonderful life without your husband. Thank you for your letter.

Misplaced Blame For Affair

DEAR ANNIE: I read your column every day, and I read with great interest the letter from the wife whose husband had an affair 20 years earlier. She was bitter that none of her friends told her about it.

I found myself in a similar situation, only I was the friend, and I DID tell her that her husband was cheating on her. This was 35 years ago.

Remember the old expression about killing the messenger? That's what happened to me. I had struggled with what to do with this information for several days. I knew she'd be devastated, but I believed she deserved the truth. She was my best friend, and I felt I'd be lying to her face every time I saw her if I didn't tell her.

I practiced for days trying to come up with the most supportive way of talking to her. I went and saw her, and we talked for about an hour, and it was very, very difficult. I left knowing that she had a lot to process and sort out, and I gave her some space. After a few days, I called but could not reach her. I left messages, but I never heard back from her.

Fifteen years later, I got a rather incoherent and angry letter from her, blaming me—for what, specifically, wasn't clear.

The wife who wrote to you complaining that no one told her might have reacted differently 20 years ago if someone had let her know. If I had had a crystal ball and known our friendship would be over if I told her, would I still have told my friend at the time? I think so. I still believe hiding it from her would have been worse, a betrayal.

—Killed Messenger in Pennsylvania

DEAR KILLED MESSENGER: Thank you for your letter. I suppose it was easier to get mad at you than her husband who had betrayed her. Just know that her meanness came out of pain and that hurt people hurt people.

Resources

BetterHelp
https://www.betterhelp.com

Couples Therapy Inc
https://www.couplestherapyinc.com

GetTested
https://gettested.cdc.gov

Grief Recovery Institute
818-907-9600
https://www.griefrecoverymethod.com

National Cervical Cancer Coalition
https://www.nccc-online.org

National Coalition Against Domestic Violence
https://ncadv.org/get-help

National Domestic Violence Hotline
800-799-7233
https://www.thehotline.org

National Help Line for Substance Abuse
800-262-2463

Sex Addicts Anonymous
https://saa-recovery.org

Sexual Recovery Anonymous
https://sexualrecovery.org

About the Author

ANNIE LANE grew up in California before heading east at the age of 18. She graduated with honors from New York University, where she majored in English literature and specialized in psychology. After NYU, she earned her Juris Doctor from New York Law School.

A lifelong learner, Annie has held a variety of jobs, including working in a law firm and for a federal magistrate. She is a certified yoga instructor with sales experience from an internet-advertising startup. Because of her great love for books and writing, Annie has also worked for Barnes & Noble and freelanced for various publications.

Since July 2016, Annie has been offering common-sense solutions to everyday problems in her internationally syndicated column, "DEAR ANNIE." Her advice is unusually perceptive. She is sympathetic, funny and firm—echoing the style of her biggest inspiration, Ann Landers.

Annie lives outside Manhattan with her husband, two kids and two dogs. When she is not writing, she devotes her time to play dates and Play-Doh.

HOW CAN I FORGIVE MY CHEATING PARTNER?
is also available as an e-book
for Kindle, Amazon Fire, iPad, Nook and Android e-readers. Visit creatorspublishing.com to learn more.

o o o

CREATORS PUBLISHING

We find compelling storytellers and
help them craft their narrative,
distributing their novels and collections
worldwide.

o o o

How Can I Forgive My Cheating Partner?

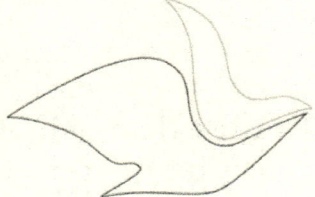

Made in the USA
Monee, IL
14 May 2022